# NYMPHENBURG

## MAIN PALACE; PARK AND PAVILIONS

### OFFICIAL GUIDE

Revised

by

GERHARD HOJER

and

ELMAR D. SCHMID

With additional material by
RAINER SCHUSTER

1999

Bayerische Verwaltung der staatlichen Schlösser,
Gärten und Seen, München

The present official guide (22nd edition) is based on the 1997 edition, with additional material by RAINER SCHUSTER, including details contributed by ERNST GÖTZ and WERNER RESCHER. Picture editor ELMAR D. SCHMID. Plan of palace and park by NORBERT NORDMANN.

*Illustrations:* Helicolor: p. 105 – W.-Chr. v. d. Mülbe: pp. 27, 29. – E. D. Schmid: pp. 54, 57, 58, 60, 61, 69, 90, 97, 108, 109. – K. v. Zabuesnig: pp. 106, 110. All others Bayerische Schlösserverwaltung.

*Cover picture:* Garden side of Nymphenburg Palace with the main canal

*translated by* Sue Bollans

22nd Edition(revised)
© 1999 by Bayerische Verwaltung der staatlichen Schlösser, Gärten und Seen, Munich
*Lay-out, typography + setting:* Frese, Munich
*Lithography:* ReproLine, Munich
*printed by:* Rother-Druck München
ISBN 3-932982-16-9
Printed in Germany

# CONTENTS

*Nymphenburg Palace*                                      *M. Wening, 1701*

# HISTORY

Nymphenburg Palace, west of their residential capital, Munich and involving a journey of approximately two hours, was the Bavarian rulers' favourite summer residence. This unusual palace complex consists of a coherent arrangement of separate cubic blocks around a central block of the same shape. On the town side building tracts projecting on either side and a crescent (Rondell) surround a spacious cour d'honneur, and on the opposite side there is an extensive park.

The complex was not all created at once. From 1664, when the foundation stone was laid, the planning, building and conversion continued until well into the 19th century. Five rulers from the Wittelsbach dynasty contributed to the creation of Nymphenburg: the Electors Ferdinand Maria, Max Emanuel, Karl Albrecht, Max III Joseph and Max IV Joseph, who became king in 1806.

## NYMPHENBURG UNDER FERDINAND MARIA AND
## HENRIETTE ADELAIDE OF SAVOY, 1663–1679

The palace was begun by Elector Ferdinand Maria who reigned from 1651–1679, and presented his consort Henriette Adelaide of Savoy with Kemnat, a farm purchased on 1.7.1663 for 10,000 florins. The occasion of this present was the birth of an heir, Max Emanuel, a year beforehand. A few days later the Electress was already writing to her mother in Turin that she wanted to build at "Kemmertin"; the plans put forward by the Turin architect Amadeus Castellamonte were too modest for her and she eventually decided in favour of designs by Agostino Barelli of Upper Italy, architect of the Munich Theatinerkirche, which was also built in honour of the young heir. In 1664 the ground was prepared for the palace, and in 1675 the roof was completed. An engraving by Michael Wening dating from 1701 (p. 4) shows the palace from the outside, which resembles the "villa suburbanas", common in Italy: a cubic block with five storeys separated by string courses. The central portal is reached via two symmetrical flights of steps, built in 1675 with the flights on the garden side, which were probably of the same design.

The extensive building activity recorded for the year 1673 was continued under Henrico Zucalli, who was commissioned to work on both the Theatinerkirche and Nymphenburg as Barelli's successor. It was only now that the stone vaulted ceiling was built; the central gables, which by then had gone out of fashion, were taken down.

The interior plan was basically as it is today. A suite of four apartments for the Elector was located opposite a suite for the Electress. The centre of the palace was the Great Hall ("Steinerner Saal"), which already had the dimensions of the present hall. On its west side, however, it was separated by a wall from an adjacent smaller hall. The Great Hall initially had smooth, plain walls with magnificent marbled stucco portals projecting from them as decorative features.

When the Electress died in 1676, work on the palace came to a stop, in spite of Elector Ferdinand Maria's decree that "the building of Nymphenburg is to be continued and completed". At the end of 1675 the stucco-worker Andreas Römer had commenced work on the interior, and submitted an estimate in 1676 for the "gilding of the partly completed and partly unfinished" ceilings.

Paintings on canvas were produced for the ceilings by the Italian artists Antonio Domenico Triva, Antonio Zanchi, Stefano Catani and the Swiss artist Joseph Werner, but not all of them were immediately installed.

At the same time as the palace was being built, a garden was laid out on the west side, of which there is a record in the engraving by Wening (p. 4). Positioned around a large fountain in the centre are four smaller pools, connected with one another by radiating paths. A semicircular wall with statue niches separates the garden at the back from the open ground beyond. This form seems to have set the pattern for the crescent which was later created on the other side of the palace. The first Nymphenburg gardens were modelled on the garden parterre at the rear of the hunting lodge Venaria Reale near Turin, which was built by Karl Emanuel II, Adelaide's brother.

## MAX EMANUEL AND NYMPHENBURG, 1679–1726

When Ferdinand Maria died, he was succeeded by his son Max Emanuel. The Turkish Wars, in which he played a dominant part as the "Blue Elector", and his role as governor of the Spanish Netherlands, which he assumed in 1692, however entailed a long absence from Munich.

### First building period under Max Emanuel

In 1701, after his return from the Netherlands, Max Emanuel once again turned his attention to Nymphenburg, and set about transforming his mother's country residence into a complex of massive proportions. The architect responsible for the building phase commencing in 1701 was Henrico Zuccalli from Roveredo in the southern Grisons, who had already established his reputation with the palaces in Lustheim and Schleißheim and the completion of the Munich Theatinerkirche. The building was supervised by his rival Antonio Viscardi, who became court architect in 1702.

Zuccalli's first move was to pull down two unfinished blocks on either side of the central building. In accordance with the requirements of Max Emanuel he then designed two residential buildings similar to the cubic block of the main building, which were constructed on either side of it and connected to it with gallery buildings. It was thus that the concept was developed on which all further additions were based, that of a loosely connected series of buildings providing openings into the park, which fundamentally distinguishes Nymphenburg from compact palaces such as Versailles.

The front of the palace, on the town side, is linked with the park not only by openings in the gallery buildings but also by the passage through the ground floor of the central building, constructed at the time so that vehicles could be driven through it.

Contrary to previous opinion, the ground plan of Nymphenburg is of Dutch rather than French origin, modelled on Ryswick Palace near The Hague (completed in 1697) and the staggered cubic blocks of Het Loo Palace (1685–1687). While he was governor, Max Emanuel had acquired an appreciation for Dutch architecture and had adopted the

7

*Elector Max Emanuel after the battle of Harsan*
*Joseph Vivien (atelier), Paris, around 1710*

ideas of the country's leading architect Daniel Marot with respect to both park (Schleißheim) and palace design. On a number of occasions his court architect Henrico Zuccalli received personal instructions from the Elector in the Netherlands, which were applied in Munich.

With the expansion of the palace complex, changes were also made in the main block. On both the town and the park side, Zuccalli inserted two rows of huge round-arched windows, one above the other, which lent a rare transparency to the original solidly designed building with its several rows of small windows. Zuccalli also used this window motif in a similar way in the New Palace in Schleißheim, having first introduced it on the façade of Ingolstadt University in 1693.

The façade of the central building at this time was divided up by lisenes, cut through by a moulding above the upper row of round-arched windows. Today this pattern is still reflected on the town side of the palace, where the massive pilasters only reach as far as this string course.

The exterior alterations to the "Great Hall" were accompanied by a major transformation of the interior. The west wall was opened on the first and second floor, thus also letting light from this side into the room. The two halls one above the other on the park side were connected with the "Great Hall" by a double row of arcades. The marbled stucco portals remained and the large room, which – including the transverse oval windows – was then already the height it is today, was additionally decorated with pilasters and the present console moulding. With these and the double rows of round-arched windows it was thus similar to the Great Hall in the New Palace of Schleißheim.

Work on the interior of the "Great Hall" commenced in September 1701. Records state that the stone masons were preparing the room for the painters from 7 to 12 October and the carpenter was paid for his contribution on 15 October. The painting of the hall was undertaken by Johann Anton Gumpp in 1701 and completed in 1703. As was appropriate for a hunting lodge and summer residence, the ceiling was decorated with scenes from the legend of Diana. As in Lustheim Palace, where Gumpp also participated in the decoration, the central painting depicted Jupiter granting Diana hunting rights. Four accompanying pictures showed the goddess as a huntress surrounded by her nymphs. There is a further reference to hunting in the oval corner paintings with Ganymede, Orion, Castor and Bellorophon. The hall walls were covered with nine huge paintings of scenes from the life of the hunting goddess Diana that reached from the moulding to the floor. In 1726 these pictures seem to have been replaced by paintings on leather, painted by the Valeriani brothers in Venice and specially ordered for the "Great Hall" by Max Emanuel.

The themes of the paintings in the "Great Hall" – as also in the hunting lodge of Lustheim – which include rare scenes from the life of Diana, are probably based on the work of the humanist at the Turin court, Emanuele Tesauro. He had already compiled a comprehensive cycle of material from the Diana legend for Venaria Reale, the hunting lodge of Adelaide's parents near Turin.

In the period from 1701 to 1703, the electoral apartments in the main building of Nymphenburg Palace also underwent alteration. According to a report by Henrico Zuccalli, from 19 April 1701 on, craftsmen and stucco-workers were at work in the apartments adjacent to the "Great Hall". On 2 November 1701, five ceilings were brought into the palace from the palace farm and hung up. These were probably the canvas paintings completed around 1675 by Triva, Zanchi, Catani and Werner, which had either been stored in the farm after the death of Ferdinand Maria (1679) or kept there during the renovation work. These paintings of ancient gods can still be seen today in the apartments on either side of the "Great Hall". In one place stucco-work from this time has also been preserved, which according to the building accounts was probably the work of Pietro F.A. Appiani from Porta near Milan.

The outbreak of the War of the Spanish Succession in 1704 caused a delay in the work on Nymphenburg. It was only when Max Emanuel returned from exile after the Rastatt Peace Treaty was concluded on 7 March 1714 that building activities could be resumed at their previous level.

*Nymphenburg Palace, town side*        *M. de Geer, around 1730*

*Second building phase under Max Emanuel*

The next building stage was the responsibility of Joseph Effner. Effner was the son of a Dachau gardener and in 1714, after completing his training in Paris, took over the Nymphenburg project. In 1715 he became an electoral court architect and in 1724 – after the death of Zuccalli – chief architect at court.

In 1714 he began to turn the lisenes of the main block into pilasters, reinforcing them on the garden side and taking them up to the eaves cornice. It was also at this time also that the number of windows flanking the large arches in the central building was reduced from four to three, as is first shown in Franz Joachim Beich's 1723 view of the palace, which hangs in the North Gallery. The older window arrangement came to light when the plastering on the façade was removed in 1971. In 1726 Charles Dubut was paid for the stucco reliefs above the windows. The central building acquired three large triangular gables (removed in 1826) above the three central axes. Effner was thus responsible for the final form of the façade.

Joseph Effner also designed the courtyards on either side of the palace complex, which were at first intended to be separate from the main palace. On the south side were the court stables with the apartments of the cavaliers (now the location of the Marstallmuseum, see official guide to the Marstallmuseum). The various sections of the building were completed in 1719, 1733 and 1747. The keystones of the arch over the driveway are marked "CA 1740" and the building is the joint work of Joseph Effner, Johann Gunezrhainer and François Cuvilliés the Elder. To balance it the Orangerie was built on the north side of the palace; the Johannis Tower at one corner had already been built in 1716. The Orangerie itself was not however completed until 1755/57.

The long façade with its separately roofed central and corner blocks and the uniform rows of blind arcades on the ground floor and segmental arched windows on the upper floor identify the buildings as an example of "modern" French architecture, of which Effner had firsthand experience when he was studying in Paris (Hôtel des Invalides) under the leading architect at the French court, Germain Boffrand. It was here that Effner also became acquainted with the new decoration form of the Régence period (strapwork). He first applied it in the ante-chamber on the north side of the main palace building, which was pan-elled by the court woodworker Johann Adam Pichler in 1720. Effner's profusion of elegant strapwork and latticework, interspersed with tro-phies of victory and emblems of the arts, laid the foundation for the dé-cor of the later Rococo period, which matured under the influence of François Cuvilliés the Elder in the 1730s in Munich and reached per-fection in the Bavarian Rococo of the 50s and 60s. One of the most im-portant workshops at the court of Max Emanuel was that of the sculp-tors, who included Guillaume de Groff from Antwerp, the Parisian sculptor Charles Dubut and the Italian Guiseppe Volpini. In charge of woodwork at the court was the woodworker, ornamental carver and gilder Johann Adam Pichler.

The artists working in Nymphenburg at the time were the popular Italian Jacopo Amigoni, the Tirolean Johann Anton Gumpp and suc-ceeding him Nikolaus Gottfried Stuber, also Franz Joachim Beich from Ravensburg and the French artists Joseph Vivien, Nicolas Bertin and François Roettier.

In the final years of Max Emanuel's life, 1723 and 1724, two-storey buildings connecting the main palace with the Marstall and Orangerie were built in place of the single-storey arcade galleries that were origi-nally planned, the "Comedihaus" was built on the south side (later re-built as the kitchen block) and a building for a ball game ("Paßspiel") and billiards on the north side. The connecting galleries across the canals were built at a later date, the "north water corridor" in 1739, and the south corridor only after Gunezrhainer took over building opera-tions in 1745. Effner was also the architect of the three garden buildings introduced in Max Emanuel's reign: in the northern half of the park the Pagodenburg in the Chinoiserie style fashionable at the time (1716–19) and in the southern half the Badenburg (1719–21), a rare example of an early 18th century bathing palace. In the last year of Max Emanuel's life Effner embarked on a hermitage, the Magdalenenklause, where the ageing Elector could retreat for devotional meditation. He did not, however, live to see it completed.

*Nymphenburg Palace, garden side*            *M. de Geer, around 1730*

Under Elector Karl Albrecht (from 1742 Karl VII, Emperor of the Holy Roman Empire) a "Carlstadt" was planned, which was almost certainly also the work of Effner. It was probably modelled on Karlsruhe, which has a similar lay-out: the palace stands in the middle of a crescent, with the streets of the town – never completed in Nymphenburg – radiating out from it. The first crescent building was constructed in 1728 on the south side (for court inspector Hieber), and the last building, which housed the porcelain manufactory (founded by Max II Joseph in 1747 in Neudeck in der Au), in 1758 on the north side. Even before the "Carlstadt" project the extensive cour d'honneur on the town side was to have been turned into a park with canals, pools, green areas and a fountain. A cour d'honneur as a garden: this idea, originating from Joseph Effner, son of a gardener, and Dominique Girard, was completely novel. According to this plan, the garden was surrounded by the crescent which, with its two-storey buildings linked by low walls, thus formed the end boundary of the extensive palace complex. The impression which the Nymphenburg cour d'honneur made on the people of the time was described in 1784 by the St Gallen monastery librarian P. Johannes Nepomuk Hauntinger as follows.

"There is an absolutely magnificent array of buildings here; together they form a completely uniform amphitheatre which is exceptionally beautiful. At the centre of this amphitheatre the splendid palace dominates all the other buildings, with entry via two grand flights of marble steps embellished with balustrades, vases and lions. Extending from both sides of this central point is a semicircle of buildings, which are all visible at once and which are perfectly symmetrical."

The planned "Carlstadt", however, involved more than just extending the palace complex with the crescent, and also included a settlement along the two drives on either side of the palace canal. This was intended for craftsmen and tradesmen, whose trade, legal rights and several years of tax exemption would be protected by the court. In return, however, they were expected to build their houses and lay out their gardens at their own expense in accordance with specific guidelines. The new settlement was also to include artists: one of the most important of those who came to live in Carlstadt being the court wood-worker Johann Adam Pichler, who was frequently required to work in the Munich Residence and Nymphenburg Palace. However, new arrivals ceased as early as the 1740s, and a few decades later this town-planning project had been forgotten.

The stables grouped around the large courtyard in the rectangular building on the south side of the palace were also a remarkable construction of extensive proportions. After the idea of the massive west tract was given up, probably at the latest with the death of Max Emanuel (the present administrative tract housing the Bavarian Department for State-owned Palaces, Gardens and Lakes dates from 1986/89), there were various projects with a more open west side where the park formed a backdrop to the courtyard. This is how, for example, it is shown in a drawing by the "court engineer" Johann Adam Zisla: the first courtyard extended into the garden in the form of an arena with a wrought-iron barrier curving round it. At the transition to the park there was to have been a flat-roofed building with five axes which, according to the legend on Zisla's drawing, was intended as a menagerie. What is certain is that the counterpart to the western wing that is shown in this spot in 18th-century veduttas was never actually built.

Karl Albrecht's favourite architect (from 1725 on) was the Walloon dwarf who had also been at Max Emanel's court and had received his professional training in Paris, François Cuvilliés the Elder. His main contribution to Nymphenburg was the little hunting lodge Amalienburg, considered to be the most perfect example of German Rococo art. Foremost among the craftsmen who contributed to the interior were the brilliant stucco worker Johann Baptist Zimmermann and the Munich woodworker Joachim Dietrich. However, the designer of the incomparably beautiful decoration was without a doubt François Cuvilliés, one of the greatest decorative artists of the century and the brilliant creator of the finest Rococo ornamentation.

Elector Max III Joseph, the last Elector of the Rococo age, was responsible for completing numerous unfinished projects in Nymphenburg, as well as in the Munich Residence and in Schleißheim. The last remaining building work was accomplished, for example in the crescent and in particular on the north wing with the Orangerie tract, which was only completed by Johann Baptist Gunezrhainer in 1755/57. On its upper floor, in addition to guest apartments (no longer in existence), was the Hubertus Hall with nine window axes, which supplemented the "Great Hall"as a "secondary" venue for ceremonial occasions and theatrical performances. Under Max III Joseph, all four park buildings were renovated and the park was decorated with the white marble statues of which there had previously been only rather random examples, often of a provisory nature. Shortly before his death, the furnishing of the "Green Hall" in the connecting tract on the south side was begun, so that it could be used as the cavaliers' dining hall; at the same time the kitchen was moved from the neighbouring building to the ground floor of the same tract.

Max III Joseph also contributed to Nymphenburg by renovating and redecorating many of the rooms. The most important room, the "Great Hall", acquired a colourful new interior appropriate to its function as a ceremonial and concert hall. In the splendid style of mature Bavarian Rococo, it was the work of Johann Baptist Zimmermann. François Cuvilliés the Elder, who returned in 1755 from his second stay in Paris, seems to have been less involved in Johann Baptist Zimmermann's design than was previously assumed; however the white wall decoration in the Garden Hall and Gallery Hall (Music Gallery) is without a doubt his work. The huge ceiling fresco in the main hall at the end of Nymphenburg's long building history once again depicted the goddess Flora and the nymphs, to whom the Electress Adelaide had dedicated her summer residence ninety years previously. François Cuvilliés the Elder was also involved in the alteration of the two corner cabinets in the palace in 1763/64. The rocaille ornamentation of the ceilings is the work of Franz Xaver Feichtmayr the Younger, who became the court stucco artist in Munich after the death of Johann Baptist Zimmermann.

A number of other artists were involved in the redecoration of the palace in the 50s and 60s. Ambrosius Hörmannstorffer decorated a number of smaller halls and cabinets with flowers or Chinese themes; woodwork and sculpture was still being supplied by the large workshop of Johann Adam Pichler, where his son and successor Joseph Adam Pichler also began working; other artists and craftsmen were the woodworkers Simon Pruckher and Tobias Grün, the woodcarver Johann Caspar Hörspucher and the sculptor Johann Thomas Sailler (carved furniture), the woodworker Johann Georg Eggerer (plain furniture), the cabinet-maker Georg Sebastian Guglhör, the respected court gilder Lorenzo Bigarello and the gilders Johann Murpöck and Johann Georg Frauenholz, the embroiderer Fr. J. A. Jansen, the metalworkers Johann Joseph Kraus and Joseph Stürzer (fire irons and metal fittings) and the grotto specialist Anton Langenburcher (glass chandeliers).

### ELECTOR KARL THEODOR, 1777–1799

Under Karl Theodor, the first Elector from the Palatinate line, the two gallery tracts between the main building and the first side blocks (1795) were widened. Although this resulted in three very pleasant rooms in each tract facing the park, the garden could no longer be seen through the gallery rooms. The façades were also completely renovated. Most importantly, Karl Theodor was responsible for summoning the Palatinate court gardener Friedrich Ludwig Sckell to Munich. By 1792 Nymphenburg Park was already open to the public, by order of the Elector.

### CHANGES UNDER MAX IV. JOSEPH, 1799–1826, FROM 1806 KING MAX I.

When Bavaria became a kingdom, King Max I, whose favourite residence was Nymphenburg and who also died here, had large sections of the palace rebuilt. The building project was begun in 1806 under the

*Nymphenburg Palace, garden side*     *Bernardo Bellotto, known as Canaletto, 1761*

direction of Karl Ludwig Puille, son of the court architect Charles Pierre Puille who died in 1805, and of Andreas Gärtner. The building records of 1806–1808 list work on the "New Rooms" for the King on the ground floor of the first block on the south side and on the "New Apartments" of the Queen on the floor above. The first block on the north side was also altered, with the loss of most of the 18th-century furnishings as a result.

In accordance with the fashion of the times, the rooms were austere and simple, but the furnishings exquisitely beautiful. The "Maserzimmer" (R. 16), the Blue Salon (R. 19) and the Bedroom (R. 20) still have their original silk coverings, sopraportas and fine furniture.

Even before the renovation of the palace, Max Joseph had engaged Friedrich Ludwig Sckell to turn the grounds into a landscaped park of the English type. With this park and the renovated rooms, Nymphenburg thus became one of the foremost residences of the early 19th century.

In 1826 the classicist style was introduced by Leo von Klenze with alterations to the central building. The gable with the coat of arms of the Bavarian electors and a massive cornice supported by wooden consoles were removed in attempt to do justice to contemporary tastes in architecture.

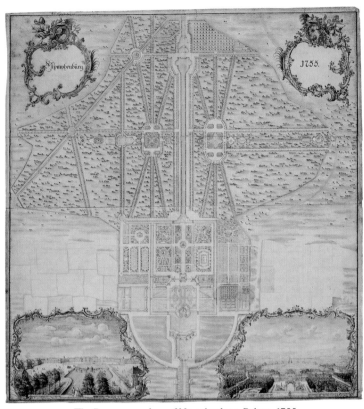

*The Baroque gardens of Nymphenburg Palace, 1755*

As a summer residence, Nymphenburg was associated from the out-set with an electoral "pleasure garden". The original grounds laid out for the electress Adelaide were still of modest proportions, but in 1701 Max Emanuel embarked on the development of one of the finest parks in Germany, summoning first Charles Carbonet, a pupil of Le Nôtre (1701) and then, more importantly, Dominique Girard (1715) from Paris for the purpose. It was then that the wide canal branching from the River Würm and entering the park by the Cascade was created to form the central axis. By 1730 this was balanced by the canal on the town side, which flows between two splendid avenues. The Cascade was de-signed by Effner. In 1731, however, Girard had what is described in the records as the "lamentable upper cascade" reconstructed in nagelfluh and "faced the surfaces over which the water flowed with marble". In 1768, under Elector Max III Joseph, the court stone mason Joseph Cajetan Linsinger began to face the entire the pool in red and grey marble.

The Large Parterre west of the palace was divided into eight sections with flower beds in the middle. At the centre was the Flora pool by Guillaume de Groff; with dragon and dolphin fountains added at a lat-er date. The lower parterre was flanked by boskets or hedge gardens, such as the summer orangery with orange trees in tubs; there was also a garden for a ball game and one for a popular Russian version of the game of nine-pins, each with little open pavilions ("cabinets à jour") and a maze with an open-air theatre enclosed by hedges.

The architectural focal points of the horizontal axis (although this was not open to view from end to end) in these geometrically designed gardens were originally the pavilions, the Pagodenburg and the Baden-burg with their parterres, playing fountains and clipped hedges. A bosket on the north side of the gardens, a "lonely and melancholy spot" was chosen as the site of the Magdalenenklause. The small pavil-ion-like building on a sketch by Franz Joachim Beich at the centre of an octagonal star opposite the Magdalenenklause, on the spot where the Amalienburg was eventually built, is almost certainly the work of Effner. The Amalienburg was also originally surrounded by a strictly geometric garden, continuing the pattern of the interior. A bow-shaped hedge enclosed the small cour d'honneur on the west side of the hunting lodge. From 1733 a wall was built round the park with gates at the ends of the main axes to direct the eye from the "manipulated" natural surroundings of the park to the open countryside beyond.

Max Emanuel had already laid out two small gardens with flowerbeds shaped in ornamental patterns next to the electoral living quarters. In 1757 the charming octagonal aviary (designed by François Cuvilliés the Elder) was built for Max III Joseph in the garden on the south side. The building was painted inside and out by Ambrosius Hörmannstorffer, and fragments of the delightful façade (repeatedly restored) still remain, featuring playing putti, bouquets of flowers in vases, garlands and flying birds. In 1768 François Cuvilliés the Younger built the "Small Cascade" in the same garden, from a design by the elder Cuvilliés. Max III Joseph also contributed to the beauty of the park by introducing a large number of marble sculptures and vases.

In the early 19th century (1804–23), the Baroque bosket gardens with their symmetrical pattern were transformed by the brilliant landscape gardener Friedrich Ludwig Sckell into the landscape garden of the type that had already been popular in England since the beginning of the 18th century. Sckell, who in one of his essays ("Beiträge zur Bildenden Gartenkunst") expresses the opinion that majestic avenues that harmonize with the architecture not only covey an impression of splendour and luxury, but are also of practical use to the people walking in the park, retained the basic features of the Baroque garden; basing his landscape garden on the Large Parterre and the central canal he thus gave his creation the unique character for which it is greatly admired.

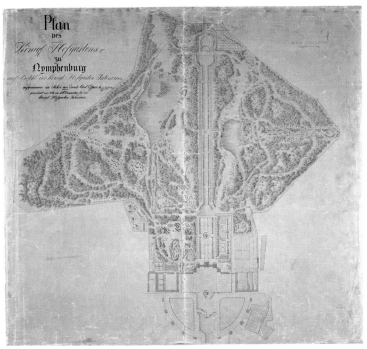

*The landscape garden of Nymphenburg Palace*
*Record of the garden as it was in 1832 by Carl Effner*

*"Great Hall" in the main palace (Room 1)*

## THE MAIN PALACE

### 1. "Great Hall" (Steinerner Saal)

In this hall the generous proportions and festive decoration combine to produce an impression of overwhelming grandeur. The architecture of the room, a framework of high pilasters with composite capitals, architrave, frieze and console moulding, was applied to the initially plain walls by Henrico Zuccalli in 1702 and decorated in 1756 by Johann Baptist Zimmermann. A further special feature of the hall is the round-arched windows on either side, which not only fill the huge room with light but also open it on the town side and, across the Garden Hall interposed at the back, to the park. Easy access to both areas is provided with external flights of steps, which were characteristic of Nymphenburg from the beginning. Since there was then no need for stairs inside, it was possible to achieve the unusual dimensions of the "Great Hall". The steps also mark the palace as a summer residence.

*Main building of Nymphenburg Palace*
*Ground plan of the first floor*

From 1755–1757, with the participation of François Cuvilliés the Elder, Max III Joseph had the Great Hall and the two adjacent halls on the garden side rebuilt. The lavish Rococo stucco-work on the walls and Zuccalli's trough vault (before 1675) featuring numerous musical motifs and, in the corners, large figures representing the four seasons with groups of putti between them bearing the symbols of the months, was produced by the elderly Johann Baptist Zimmermann in 1755/56. He was also responsible for the green- and red-tinted grisaille painting on the ceiling fresco; the agreement with Zimmermann was signed on 18 October 1755 and the work was finished in 1757/58. The master was assisted by his son Franz Michael and his pupil Martin Heigl was responsible for many of the wall and ceiling frescos, receiving court protection in 1757 as a reward for his work.

In order to emphasize the connection with the garden, the "park landscape" was continued in the frescos, with scenes reflecting the Arcadian character of Nymphenburg. The large ceiling fresco has peace and reconciliation as its themes. In 1745 Max III Joseph laid the foundation for the regeneration of economic prosperity in his electorate with the special peace treaty of Füssen. This is underlined in the fresco with the depiction of a cultivated and flourishing "Arcadia". The reign of this peace-loving Elector marked the return of the golden age. The colour scheme of the hall is particularly attractive with white and gold for the architectural framework and a delicate green for the wall panels as the background to the colourful wall paintings, these in turn forming a transition to the colour symphony of the ceiling fresco. The gilding was under the direction of Lorenzo Bigarello, who had already been active at the court for several decades.

Large ceiling fresco by Johann Baptist Zimmermann 1755/57. On the park side of the large ceiling painting nymphs pay homage to the goddess Flora, an allegorical reference to the name of the palace, over them in the centre Apollo's sun chariot and other Olympian gods; to the left a Venus group, opposite, Diana, goddess of hunting. The dominant figure in this group is Mercury with the trumpet of Fama. On the town side of the ceiling fresco are Orpheus and Minerva instructing the muses and the drunken Bacchus under his tent. Orpheus is a direct reference to the Bavarian Elector's love of music. The figure of the vir-

*"Great Hall" in the main palace (Room 1), ceiling painting*

ginal goddess Astraea on the park side, bottom left, who only intended to come back to earth with the return of the "golden age", indicates that the ceiling painting is a glorification of the regime of Max III Joseph.

On the side walls, the central pictures on the left-hand side show Cephalus and Procris, those on the right-hand side Mars and Venus, while above the doors are pastoral scenes as allegories of the four humours. The theme of "A prosperous and flourishing country in the time of peace – return of the golden age" dealt with comprehensively in the paintings is continued in the stucco figures above the cornice.

It was probably at the end of 1756 that François Cuvilliés the Elder was requested to design the inner door pediments and the stucco décor of the white annex rooms on the main and gallery floors. The work was carried out by Zimmermann's workshop, the last order received after decoration of the Wieskirche, Schäftlarn and Maria Brünnlein near Wemding. Zimmermann's ceiling pictures in these two rooms are divided into smaller sections than the large main fresco.

On the ceiling of the Garden Hall: the abduction of Flora by Zephyr. On the pillars stucco reliefs of ancient gods. – Above on the ceiling of the music gallery: Latona and the Lycian peasants – transformation of the peasants into frogs, from Ovid's Metamorphoses. The section of wall with realistically sculptured reliefs of numerous musical instruments is particularly impressive: Elector Max III Joseph was a great music-lover who played the gamba and composed.

The "Great Hall" was never completely renovated after it was finished in 1758. Further action was limited to dusting and small improvements within the reach of the users, so that it has been preserved in its authentic Rococo form. The restoration work in 1990/95 was again limited to cleaning and filling and retouching cracks and gaps that had appeared. The six classicistic crystal chandeliers made in around 1810 with twelve matching sconces were also hung up again at this time; they were first installed in place of the seven original Rococo chandeliers when Bavaria became a kingdom.

*Furniture and fittings:* 2 console tables, Johann Adam Pichler, Munich, around 1725.
6 taborets
2 Old Imari vases, Japan, around 1700.
6 chandeliers and 12 sconces.

*Garden Hall adjoining the "Great Hall" (Room 1), ceiling painting*

## NORTH WING

Both the apartment in the central building and the group of rooms in the first block on the north side (known since the 19th century as the Crown Prince Building) that are accessible from the North Gallery contained the official apartments of the Elector. (The rooms in the north building are not open). They were entered through the First Antechamber.

## 2  First Antechamber

The gold-and-white wooden panelling was carved entirely in the French Régence style by the court woodworker and flower carver Johann Adam Pichler, who received his training in Paris.

The panelled ceiling was completed in around 1675 during the first building period of the palace: in the central oval is Ceres on a chariot pulled by dragons, painted by Antonio Zanchi; in the corner panels are putti bearing the gifts of Ceres, painted by Johann Anton Gumpp.

*Painting: Sopraportas:* Children at play as allegories of the four elements by Jacopo Amigoni, 1716. On the back wall a portrait of Elector Max Emanuel as a commander with the fortress of Namur in the background, by Joseph Vivien, 1711. Opposite the fireplace a portrait of Max Emanuel's second wife, Therese Kunigunde of Poland, by Franz Joseph Winter after an original by Vivien.

*Furnishings:* Console table, Johann Adam Pichler, Munich, around 1725.

Commode, around 1740.

Mantelpiece clock, H. v. Soest (signature on the clock face) and Gosselin (clockwork), Paris, around 1720.

2 Old Imari vases decorated with figures, Japan around 1700.

## 3     *Second Antechamber (Tapestry Room)*

Baroque panelled ceiling painted in the early 18th century by Johann Anton Gumpp: The Triumph of Stratagem, Mars and Minerva above the Trojan Horse.

*Tapestries:* On the rear wall, Diana from a series "The Triumphs of the Gods", Brussels around 1720, the combined work of Heinrich Reydams and Urban and Daniel Leyniers from a design by Jan van Orley and Augustin Coppens. On the side walls March – April and July – August from a series of garden scenes illustrating the months, Brussels, around 1690, by Jan Frans van den Hecke.

*Paintings:* Sopraportas: Two still-lifes with flowers and fruits, 18th century. Over the fireplace: portrait of Max Emanuel's second wife, Therese Kunigunde of Poland, portrayed as Venus with Cupid; painted by Martin Maingaud.

*Furnishings:* Writing table (bureau plat) with bronze fittings, Paris, around 1750/60.

2 console tables, signed by Adam Weisweiler, Paris, around 1785.

Seating signed by Georges Jacob, Paris, around 1780 (probably originally from Karlsberg Palace near Zweibrücken).

2 pairs of girandoles, each with three candles, around 1810.

## 4   Former Bedroom

Baroque panelled ceiling with paintings. – Central picture: the sea goddess Thetis, enthroned on a shell in the clouds. Painted by the Swiss artist Joseph Werner (attributed to J. Glaesemer), 1672/73. Identical with a painting by Werner mentioned in Sandrart's Academy, where he "...portrayed Thetis, in the heavens and surrounded by many charming gods, throwing down from her chariot many rare seashells, to the complete satisfaction of your Electoral Highness". A sketch for this is in the copperplate cabinet of the Berlin State Museums.

Wall-panelling renewed in the 19th century. The rear wall was recovered in blue damask in 1966.

*Paintings: Sopraportas:* Diana in Repose and Toilet of Venus, 18th-century replicas after François Boucher. By the fireplace: Elector Max Emanuel after the Battle of Harsan, atelier of Joseph Vivien, Paris, around 1710. Elector Max III working at a lathe with the Count of Salern, Johann Jakob Dorner, 1765.

On the rear wall in a carved gilt Rococo frame: Conversation Piece. The Bavarian and Saxon electoral families making music and playing cards: 32 small figures.

Signed and dated on the bottom left by Peter Horemans, 1761.

Prince Friedrich Christian of Saxony visited his brother-in-law Max III Joseph of Bavaria between 1760 and 1762 with his family and court. The painting records a concert and a game of cards, which took place as court entertainment in Nymphenburg. According to the inventory of 1763, the picture hung at that time in the Elector's apartments.

*The musicians in the left half of the picture:* Elector Clemens August of Cologne, died 1761, on the bass viol, Marchioness Maria Josepha of Baden, sister of Max III Joseph,

*Painting of the Bavarian and Saxon electoral families (detail) P.J. Horemans, 1761 (Room 4)*

*Painting of the Bavarian and Saxon electoral families (detail)*
*P.J. Horemans, 1761 (Room 4)*

at the harpsichord and Prince Karl of Saxony playing the flute. Princess Elisabeth of Saxony is the singer and Duke Clemens Franz of Bavaria in a blue deer-hunter's uniform is conducting. The crippled Prince Friedrich Christian, wearing the order of the Polish white eagle, is listening from his invalid chair. The members of the Bavarian Electoral family are wearing the order of St George.

*Card-players left of centre (from left to right);* Princess Christina of Saxony; Cardinal and Duke Johann Theodor of Bavaria, an uncle of the Bavarian Elector; Princess Josepha of Bavaria, a sister of the Elector, later the wife of Emperor Joseph II; Elector Max III Joseph of Bavaria. – In the background, forming a link between the first and second group, Maria Anna, Electress of Bavaria with her brother Prince Xaver of Saxony.

*Group of people drinking coffee at the right-hand edge of the picture:* Maria Anna, Duchess of Bavaria; Princess Kunigunde of Saxony and Maria Antonia, née Princess of Bavaria, a sister of the Bavarian Elector and wife of Prince Friedrich Christian of Saxony.

*On the left-hand wall:* Max Emanuel's Little Gallery of Beauties from the Elector's bedroom on the upper floor of the Badenburg, that was destroyed in 1944. 9 portraits of ladies at the court of Louis XIV, some disguised as goddesses, painted by Pierre Gobert in around 1715 for the Elector, who during his exile lived from 1713 on in St. Cloud near Paris: (from top to bottom and from left to right) two unknown ladies, Princess de Brissac as Diana, Duchess of Luxembourg, Mademoiselle de Clermont with a dog, Madame de Ville Franche as Flora, Mademoiselle de la Motte with globe and eagle. Princess Conti with torch and Cupid, Countess Polignac as Pomona (her old servant as Vertumnus).

*Furnishings:* Stope-front (bureau en pente) with "butterfly wing" inlaid work, Paris, around 1750, attributed to Jean Dubois.

Collapsible travel writing desk belonging to Count Seeau, inscribed 1772, Paris, around 1750.

Console table, signed by Georges Jacob, Paris 1781/82 (originally from Karlsberg Palace near Zweibrücken).

Seating signed by Georges Jacob, Paris, around 1780 (originally also from Karlsberg palace).

33

## 5  North Cabinet

The northern corner cabinet acquired its present form under the supervision of François Cuvilliés the Elder in 1763/64, when it was reduced in size and the ceiling was newly decorated with stucco-work by Franz Xaver Feichtmayr the Younger. In the corners are rocaille cartouches with putti as allegories of the four seasons. The naturalistic stucco-work was restored in its original form in 1950/51.

*Paintings:* Heads from ancient mythology, around 1775–80.

*Furnishings:* Writing-desk with a semicircular closure (bureau à cylindre) around 1775–80; marquetry with musical instruments.

Chandelier with twelve candles, around 1770.

## 6  Max Emanuel's Gallery of Beauties

The three rooms on the garden side of the North Gallery were created when the gallery tract was enlarged by Elector Karl Theodor in 1795. They were redecorated in 1967.

*Paintings:* Max Emanuel's Great Gallery of Beauties, five portraits of ladies at the court of Louis XIV, painted by Pierre Gobert in around 1715, at the same time as the portraits in the Little Gallery of Beauties (Room 4). From left to right: Princesse de Conti (daughter of Louis XIV and the Marquise de Montespan) with Cupid, Mademoiselle de Charolois, Duchesse de Berry, Mademoiselle de Clermont, Marquise de Gondrin with Cupid. View of the Magdalenenklause, Franz Joachim Beich, around 1725/30.

*Furnishings:* Commode, Munich, around 1740/50, probably from an original by Bernard II Vanrisamburgh.

Console table, Munich, around 1750/55.

6 chairs, signed by Georges Jacob, Paris, 1781–82.

Mirror, Johann Caspar Hörspurcher, around 1750, probably from a design by François Cuvilliés the Elder.

Mirror, around 1765, attributed to Johann Thomas Sailler.

2 sconces, around 1750.

Chandelier in this room and the two neighbouring rooms around 1775 (originally in the "Green Hall" in the South Wing of the palace).

Mantelpiece clock, Europa mounted on the bull, with the maker's name: "Millot. Hger Du Roy, à Paris", Paris, around 1750/55.

## 7 Room with Coat-of-Arms Tapestries

*Marble busts:* Elector Karl Theodor as Hercules and his first wife Elisabeth Auguste of Pfalz-Sulzbach as Minerva, around 1780.

*Paintings: Sopraportas:* Still-lifes with poultry, crayfish, fruit and vegetables, 18th century; two still-lifes with fruit, signed by Johann Amandus Wink, 1795.

*Tapestries:* 4 tapestries with the combined coat-of-arms of the Kurpfalz (Electorate of the Palatinate) and Pfalz-Sulzbach of Elector Karl Theodor and his first wife Elisabeth Auguste, Stephan Boßmann / Savonnerie manufactory Heidelberg-Mannheim, from 1756.

*Furnishings:* 2 guéridons (candelabra stands), Paris, around 1785.

4 armchairs, signed by Georges Jacob, Paris 1781–82.

3 sconces, Johann Thomas Sailler, Munich 1766.

## 8 Karl Theodor Room

*Paintings:* Portraits of the Elector Karl Theodor as Grand Master of the Order of St George and of his first wife Elisabeth Auguste of Pfalz-Sulzbach, signed and dated on the bottom left by Anton Hickel. fecit: 1780; the frames are attributed to the sculptor Augustin Egell. – On the window wall a portrait of the second wife of Elector Karl Theodor, Maria Leopoldine of Austria-Este, signed by Joseph Hauber, 1797.

*Furnishings:* Console table, Munich, last quarter of the 18th century.

2 guéridons (candelabra stands), signed by Georges Jacob, Paris, 1780–81 (probably from Karlsberg Palace near Zweibrücken); standing on them 2 girandoles, probably by Gouthière, Paris (?) around 1780.

6 chairs, signed by Georges Jacob, Paris 1781–82, coverings from 1867 (from Karlsberg Palace near Zweibrücken).

Wall mirror, around 1780.

*Chair from Karlsberg Palace
Jacob, Paris 1781/82 (Room 8)*

## 9    North Gallery

Corridor leading to the Elector's apartment (not accessible) in the first building on the north side of the main block. Interior decoration from the time of Max Emanuel. Large pictures of Nymphenburg Palace set in panels on the wall and decorated with elaborate carved ornamentation by Johann Adam Pichler. These veduttas, painted by Franz Joachim Beich in 1722/23, are a valuable record of the original concept and appearance of the palace and gardens.

The views are as follows:

*On the first window pillar on the right:* Nymphenburg Palace from the garden side.

*Opposite:* Front view of Nymphenburg Palace with the French gardens and the pavilions in the background. The Amalienburg and the Magdalenenklause were added in by Joseph Stephan in 1760.

*On the second window pillar:* The hunting lodge of Fürstenried. In the foreground a hunting party with a small portrait of Elector Max Emanuel.

*Opposite:* The Badenburg. The little bathing palace with its ornate bathing hall was a completely new conception. It is portrayed in the middle of its original French-style Baroque garden with pool, clipped hedges and boskets.

*On the third window pillar:* Starnberg Palace and the electoral flotilla, dominated by the state galley of Ferdinand Maria and his wife Adelaide, the "Bucentoro", which was modelled by its builder, the Italian Santurini, on the state galley of the Doge of Venice in the 17th century.

*Opposite:* The famous Flora pool in the Large Parterre with the Flora group in gilt lead by Guillaume de Groff (1719), which disappeared after it was removed in the early 19th century.

*On the fourth window pillar:* Berg Palace on Lake Starnberg, favourite residence of the Elector Ferdinand Maria and his wife Adelaide. In the foreground a stag hunt in the lake. It was near Berg Palace that King Ludwig II, who was born in Nymphenburg Palace (R. 20), was drowned on 13 June 1886.

*Opposite:* The Cascade in Nymphenburg Park, still in existence today; the architectural setting was never built.

*Over the north door:* The Pagodenburg with the quatrefoil fountain pool of the original French garden.

*Over the south door:* The Badenburg.

## 10    First Antechamber

Access to the Electress' apartments. Under Elector Max III Joseph the red wall covering was replaced with the present panelling, decorated in gold and white. The Baroque ceiling from the first building period of the palace is decorated with paintings by Antonio Domenico Triva, with the water nymph Arethusa in the centre.

*Paintings: Sopraportas:* landscapes by Dominicus Nollet, around 1720. On the walls a portrait of Karl Albrecht as Emperor Karl VII and of his wife Maria Amalia as Empress, both from the atelier of George Desmarées.

*Furnishings:* Console table, Johann Adam Pichler, Munich, around 1725.

Commode, around 1765.

Table clock, Gillé l'ainé, Paris, around 1760.

## 11    Second Antechamber

Baroque panelled ceiling with paintings by Antonio Domenico Triva, around 1675, with the earth goddess Cybele in the centre. – Over the marble fireplace a carved mirror frame, around 1760/70.

The red damask wall covering was recreated in its original form when the room was restored in 1966.

*Paintings: Sopraportas:* two still-lifes with putti reliefs, signed by Johann Amandus Wink, 1795. – On the rear wall a double portrait of the palace's founders, Elector Ferdinand Maria and Henriette Adelaide of Savoy, 1666, attributed to Sebastiano Bombelli. – On the side walls, allegorical portraits of the palace's founders, signed by Stefano Catani, around 1675. The original oval ceiling paintings, some of the oldest decorations in Henriette Adelaide's Nymphenburg summer villa, were removed when the corner cabinets were redesigned in 1763. The northern corner cabinet originally had a portrait of Elector Ferdinand Maria as Jupiter with astronomy instruments as a patron of the arts and sciences, and the southern corner cabinet had a portrait of Electress Henriette Adelaide as Diana with her children: Maria Anna as Juno, Clemens Kajetan as Apollo and Violante Beatrix as Flora; on the right Max Emanuel, who, as the future great commander, is being presented with a sword.

*Second Antechamber in the south section of the main palace (Room 11)*

*Bedroom in the
Electress' apartment
(Room 12)*

*Furnishings:* Richly ornamented table in Italian pietra dura work, with birds and tendrils in multicoloured semiprecious stones on black marble, second half of the 17th century.

2 commodes with gilt bronze fittings, Paris, around 1730/40, attributed to E. Doirat.

4 chairs and 4 taborets, Munich, around 1760/65.

6 sconces, Johann Thomas Sailler, Munich 1766.

## 12   Bedroom

Baroque panelled ceiling with paintings by Antonio Domenico Triva, around 1675, with the goddess Flora in the centre. – Carved ornamental panel above the fireplace in the Régence style from around 1720, Rococo mirror frame on the window wall, around 1760/70. Bed baldachin with silver embroidery on green silk, around 1730.

The green damask wall covering was recreated in its original form when the room was restored in 1963.

*Chinese Lacquer
Cabinet
(Room 13)*

*Paintings: Sopraportas:* four Italian landscapes with ruins and shepherds in the foreground by Joseph Stephan, 1766. – Above the fireplace an allegorical representation of the return of the Elector Max Emanuel from exile, 1715, by François Roettier. – On the entrance wall a portrait of Max Emanuel and his sister Maria Anna as children, 1666, attributed to Sebastiano Bombelli. – On the rear wall portraits of Elector Max Emanuel and his second wife Therese Kunigunde, signed by Johann Andreas Wolff, 1704.

*Furnishings:* Secretary richly decorated with inlaid work showing rustic scenes from Holland and flowers, signed by Jean-Baptist Saunier, Paris, around 1760.

2 commodes, around 1775.

Console table, Munich, around 1750/1755.

2 chairs, around 1740/1750.

2 vases (white marble) with candelabra in the form of carved foliage.

## 13 Chinese Lacquer Cabinet

The south corner cabinet was redesigned in 1763/64 under the supervision of François Cuvilliés the Elder, and, as in the North Cabinet, the ceiling was decorated with stucco-work by Franz Xaver Feichtmayr. In the corners rocaille cartouches with putti as allegories of the four elements. The large panels of the white walls are faced with Coromandel lacquer (lacquer on a clay foundation), probably from 17th century Chinese screens. In the correct order they relay the plot of a 16th-century Chinese novel. These are complemented in the small panels by lacquer paintings with Chinese motifs by Johann Georg Hörringer. On the door wings and panels are Italian commedia dell'arte figures.

*Furnishings:* Secrétaire en pente (slope-front writing desk), Paris, around 1730/33.

Small cabinet faced with Japanese lacquer, signed by Claude-Charles Saunier, Paris, around 1780.

2 guéridons with dancing Chinese figures, Paris (?), around 1720.

## 14 South Gallery

Corridor leading to the Electress' apartment, not completed until around 1760. The panelling is much simpler than that of the North Gallery.

Paintings by Franz Joachim Beich, Nikolaus Gottfried Stuber and Joseph Stephan.

*On the first window pillar on the left:* The New Palace of Schleißheim from the garden side, painted by Franz Joachim Beich, with Effner's Baroque façade. In the background an idealized representation of the Old Palace and home farm.

*Opposite:* View of the palaces of Schleißheim by Nikolaus Gottfried Stuber. In the foreground the Old Palace, built by Elector Maximilian I in the early 17th century (badly damaged in the Second World War, the exterior reconstructed in 1971/72 and the interior in 1985/88). The New Palace of Max Emanuel is shown here with its late Baroque façade, which was altered by Leo von Klenze in 1819. The planned galleries connecting the Old and New Palaces were never built, nor was the Old Palace remodelled in the Baroque style, as shown here. In the background the palace gardens with Lustheim (built in 1684–87).

*On the second window pillar:* Lustheim from the east, painted by Franz Joachim Beich (somewhat idealized).

*East-Asian lacquered wall panel from the Chinese Lacquer Cabinet
(Room 13)*

*Opposite:* Front view of the little garden palace of Lustheim by Franz Joachim Beich. It is surrounded by a semicircular gallery, which was never fully completed and was taken down again in 1750. In the background the Lustheim canal and the canal connecting it with the River Isar.

*On the third window pillar:* Lichtenberg Palace on the River Lech, which was destroyed in the 19th century, painted by Franz Joachim Beich; it was built for Max Emanuel by Henrico Zuccalli as a hunting lodge in the early 18th century. In the foreground, heron hawking.

*Opposite:* Landshut, painted by Franz Joachim Beich, with St Martin's Church, an outstanding example of Bavarian late Gothic architecture. Above the town Trausnitz Castle, the ancestral seat of the Wittelsbachs.

*On the fourth window pillar:* View of Haag Palace east of Munich, by Joseph Stephan, 1756.

*Opposite:* The four-wings of Dachau Palace with its "hanging" gardens, painted by Franz Joachim Beich. All but the present single wing of the palace was pulled down in the early 19th century (see official guide to Dachau Palace).

*Above the entrance:* Isareck Palace, by Joseph Stephan, 1757.

*Above the exit:* Kling Palace near Wasserburg, by Joseph Stephan, 1757.


SOUTH BLOCK

On the first floor of this building were the apartments of first the Electresses, and after 1806 the Queens of Bavaria. From Elector Karl Albrecht onwards, the ruler had a private apartment on the ground floor, although he officially resided in the north tract of the palace.

## 15    King Ludwig I's Gallery of Beauties

In 1807 alterations were made on the first floor of this building to create apartments for Queen Caroline, the consort of King Max I Joseph. The gold-and-white room with its stucco-work sopraportas was originally used as a small dining room and was redesigned by Andreas Gärtner, father of the architect Friedrich von Gärtner. Today the Gallery of Beauties of King Ludwig I (who reigned from 1825–1848), which was originally intended for the Festsaalbau of the Munich Residence, is displayed here.

*Caroline Countess of Holnstein (Room 15), J Stieler, 1834*

Joseph Stieler was commissioned by the king to paint the famous series of beautiful women, not only ladies at the court as in Max Emanuel's Gallery of Beauties (Room 4) but women from all classes of society. From 1827 – 1850 he produced 36 portraits, of which one (Luise Baroness von Neubeck) was lost, and in 1861, after Stieler's death, Friedrich Dürck added two more (Carlotta von Breidbach-Bürresheim and Anna Greiner). The best known is probably the "Schöne Münchnerin" (Munich Beauty) Helene Seldmayr, daughter of a shoemaker, and the "Spanish" dancer Lola Montez, cause of the revolution in 1848, when Ludwig I was forced to abdicate.

*North wall, left*

1 Friederica Catharina, known as Wilhelmine Sulzer, married name Schneider (born 1820), painted 1838

2 Lady Emily Milbanke, née Lady Mansfield (1822–1870), painted 1844

3 Marianna Marchesa Florenzi, née Countess Baccinetti (1802–1870), painted 1831

4 Regina Daxenberger, married name von Fahrenbacher (1811–1827), painted 1829

5 Lady Jane Ellenborough (1807–1881), painted 1831

6 Amalie von Schintling (1812–1831), painted 1831

*North wall, right*

1 Mathilde Baroness von Jordan, married name Countess von Beust (1817–1886), painted 1837

2 Elise List, married name Pacher von Theinburg (1822–1893), painted 1844

3 Charlotte von Hagn, married name von Owen (1809–1891), painted 1828

4 Irene Marchioness of Pallavicini, married name Countess Arco-Steppberg (1811–1877), painted 1834

*Amalie von Schintling*
*King Ludwig I's Gallery of Beauties*
*(Room 15)*
*J. Stieler, 1831*

5 Lady Therese Spence, née Renard (born 1815), painted 1837

6 Helene Sedlmayr, married name Miller (1813–1898), painted 1831

*South wall, left*

1 Josepha Conti, née Reh (1822–1910), painted 1844

2 Carlotta Baroness von Breidbach-Bürresheim, married name Countess Boss-Waldeck (1838–1920), painted 1861

3 Caroline Lizius, married name Stobäus (1825–after 1904), painted 1842

4 Caroline Countess von Holnstein aus Bayern, née Baroness von Spiering (1815–1859), painted 1834

5 Lady Jane Erskine, married name Callander (1818–1846), painted 1837

6 Antonia Wallinger, married name von Ott (1823–1893), painted 1840

*South wall, right*

1 Creszentia Princess von Öttingen-Öttingen-Wallerstein, née Bourgin (1806–1853), painted 1833

2 Sophie Archduchess of Austria, born Princess of Bavaria, sister of King Ludwig I (1805–1872), painted 1841

3 Nanette Kaula, married name Heine (1812–1877), painted 1829

4 Catharina Botzaris, married name Karadjas (1820–1875), painted 1841

5 Friederike Baroness von Gumppenberg (baron's daughter), married name Baroness von Gumppenberg (1823–1916), painted 1843

6 Marie, Queen of Bavaria, née Princess of Prussia, mother of King Ludwig II (1825–1889), painted 1843

*West wall, left*

1 Maximiliane Borzaga, married name Krämer (1806–1837), painted 1827

2 Auguste Ferdinande Princess of Bavaria, née Archduchess of Austria, wife of the Prince Regent Luitpold of Bavaria (1825–1875), painted 1845

3 Caroline Countess von Waldbott-Bassenheim, née Princess von Öttingen-Öttingen-Wallerstein (1824–1889), painted 1843

4 Alexandra Amalia Princess of Bavaria, daughter of Ludwig I (1826–1875), painted 1845

5 Lola Montez, née Gilbert (1818–1862), painted 1847

6 Maria Dietsch, married name Sprecher (1835–1869), painted 1850

1 Rosalie Julie Baroness von Bonar, née Baroness von Wüllersdorf-Urbair (born 1814), painted 1840
2 Amalie Baroness von Kruedener, née Countess von Lerchenfeld, later married name Countess von Adlerberg (1808–1888), painted 1828
3 Auguste Strobel, married name Hilber (1807–1871), painted 1827
4 Isabella Countess Tauffkirchen-Guttenberg-Engelburg, married name Countess Kwilecky (1808–1855), painted 1828
5 Anna Hillmayer (1812–1847), painted 1829
6 Cornelia Vetterlein, married name Baroness von Künsberg (1812–1862); painted 1828

## 16 "Maserzimmer"

This room was first furnished in 1810 and restored in 1959/60, when the green silk wall covering was also renewed. Two sopraporta paintings with Pompeian motifs.

*Paintings:* Portraits of King Ludwig I and his consort Therese, by Heinrich Wilhelm E. Vogel, 1841, after Joseph Stieler.

*Furnishings:* Secretary, writing table, console tables and seating in grained cherry and birch wood, probably from Vienna, around 1810.

Table, Munich, around 1820/30.

Four chairs, Munich, around 1800.

## 17 Cabinet

The cabinet adjacent to the "Maserzimmer" has delicate grotesquerie decoration by Ambrosius Hörmannstorffer dating from 1775. The room was reduced in size on the south side and the decoration completed in the same style after 1900.

*Furnishings:* Table, around 1725

Pendule, Paris, around 1745, with Chinese figure and dragon of gilt bronze.

47

## 18   Small Gallery

The southern gallery continues with the Small Gallery of the south block, which has a view of the Small Cascade in the little cabinet garden.

*Paintings:* On the side walls two large still-lifes from the Jan Fyt school, mid 17th century.

Portrait of Anna Greiner, Friedrich Dürck, 1861. Portrait of Carlotta von Breidbach-Bürresheim, Friedrich Dürck, 1861.

*Furnishings:* 2 tables, with lion's head masks and red marble tops, around 1775.


## 19   Blue Salon

The blue silk covering of this salon designed by Andreas Gärtner was recreated in its original form when the room was restored in 1959/60.

*Painting:* Portrait of King Max I Joseph, Munich, around 1810.

*Furnishings:* The console tables, commodes and seating from around 1810 and a small, richly inlaid table with Egyptian themes, Paris, around 1810, were all part of the original furnishings.

2 porcelain vases with battle scenes (Lofer, November 1805 and Austerlitz, December 1805), Paris 1806 or 1810.


## 20   Queen's Bedroom

This room was furnished at the same time as the Blue Salon by Andreas Gärtner, and the green silk wall covering was recreated in its original form when the bedroom was restored in 1959/60. Two soraporta paintings with Pompeian motifs.

King Ludwig II (reigned from 1864–1886) was born in this room on 25 August 1845.

*Furnishings:* Bed, commodes, mirror, table and mahogany seating with bronze fittings, around 1810.

Clock with 4 black columns on the mantelpiece.

Plaster busts: Crown Prince Ludwig and Prince Otto of Bavaria, Johann Halbig, modelled in 1850.


48

*Queen's Bedroom (Room 20)*
*Birthplace of King Ludwig II of Bavaria*

## 21 Palace Chapel

(Separate entrance from the cour d'honneur in the second north block; accessible in the summer season during palace opening hours).

The chapel, in the second north block, the "Kapellenstock", was begun in 1702 by Antonio Viscardi from a design by Henrico Zuccalli. It is basically a rectangular room with a stone vault on two-and-a-half floors, an altar apsis on the north side, and above it a choir and organ balcony with a flat ceiling, specified in this form by the Elector. On the first floor at the south end are balconies for the cavaliers. On the west side above a low side aisle, the length of three window axes, is the Elector's oratory that was the obligatory feature of court chapels, separated from the rest of the chapel by windows. Above it is a second oratory.

With the Spanish War of Succession building was interrupted for more than a decade – up until then only the main walls and the roof had been completed. Elector Max Emanuel issued an order from his exile that the chapel room was to be finished in a simplified form by the time he returned. When it was consecrated in 1715, the room had Corinthian pilasters and simple stucco-work on the ceiling, and an elaborate stucco ceiling in the oratory on the first floor by F. Marazzi. The basic form of the high altar had been constructed, provisionally in white, and the oak pews and confessionals were probably also already in place. The latter indicate that the ground floor of the chapel was accessible from the beginning to the general population as well as the court. The present palace chapel in fact officially replaced the small St Magdalene's Chapel a little to the south, which was already mentioned in the 14th century and was pulled down in 1702 when the palace was first extended (see illustration p. 4). A few years after the consecration, the chapel walls were decorated with more elaborate stucco-work under the supervision of Joseph Effner and the main altar was completed. Alterations and additions continued to be made until the late 19th century. In 1987/91 the church was thoroughly restored, and the protective screen at the back is also from this time.

The frescos on the vault are by the Tirolean Joseph Mölck, who signed them "Joseph Mölckh Churfürstl: / Cammer = Mahler / 1759".

*The Nymphenburg Palace Chapel in the second north block*

*The repentent Mary Magdalene, ceiling painting in the Palace Chapel
by J. Mölck, 1759*

The picture at the back shows the repentant Mary Magdalene, while the main picture illustrates the meal in the house of Simon the Pharisee. In the spandrels are representations of the Four Evangelists: The other spandrels and the lunettes are decorated with ornamental painting.

On the altar, below the combined coat-of-arms of Bavaria and Poland (Therese Kunigunde, the second wife of Max Emanuel, was a daughter of the Polish King Johann Sobieski), is a carving of Christ appearing to Mary Magdalene as a gardener. This high-quality work, which in the 18th century was provisionally finished in white, acquired its present colours in around 1860. The life-sized figures, which are undoubtedly from the first third of the 17th century, are now attributed to Christoph Angermair (died 1632 or 1633); they were previously thought to be the work of the sculptor Andreas Faistenberger. In around 1750/60 the richly gilded late Rococo tabernacle with reliquaries on either side was placed in front of the altar; it was probably designed by François Cuvilliés the Elder and made by the Ignaz Günther school.

In the side chapel the altar retable (probably from a design by Joseph Effner) has a painting of St Hubertus by Johann Kaspar Sing. The whole altar retable was raised when the reliquary shrine with the inscription "St. PROTHI M." was added in 1735/40. The reliquary is decorated with an elaborately carved gilt frame with two putti, from around 1740, from its style probably the work of Joachim Dietrich. – Large stone sculpture of St John of Nepomuk, which in 1732 was initially placed in front of the Johannis Well House by the north side wing of the palace and was transferred to the church in 1828. In front of the altar mensa a ledger of the last member of the Gaßner family, who originally owned the farm.

The relief on the pulpit by Konrad Eberhard, added in the early 19th century, shows the Sermon on the Mount. – Font, numerous paintings and the stations of the Cross, some with richly ornamented frames, from the 18th century. Present organ from 1859/60.

On the pillar opposite the pulpit, a brass cross with an aureole and the figure of Christ in ivory, 18th century, originally in Duke Max Castle in the centre of Munich. – Below, Our Lady of Sorrows, 19th century.

*Landscape garden with bridge by the Pagodenburg*

## THE PARK

The route described below goes right round the park. It begins south of the outside steps at the back of the palace and ends in the north by the entrance to the park. A shorter route passing the Amalienburg, Badenburg, Pagodenburg and Magdalenenklause, in that order, can also be taken to visit the miniature palaces. These are described on pages 67 to 102.

From the steps at the back of the palace there is a good view of the entire park, around 500 acres in area, with the Large Parterre, the central canal ending in the Cascade (in the direction of the Pipping church tower) and the two diagonal vistas (towards Blutenburg and Pasing) of the original Baroque garden. The axes terminate in ha-has, where the surrounding wall (built mainly between 1730 and 1740) was sunk, "harmoniously linking the external landscape with that of the park" (Sckell, 1809). On either side of the central canal are the areas redesigned by Friedrich Ludwig Sckell in the English garden style with picturesque lakes, Badenburg Lake in the southern half and Pagodenburg Lake in the northern half. On the Badenburg side a canal flows out of the lake which was constructed to look "natural", "overhung and adorned with greenery" (Sckell, 1809).The outlet from Pagodenburg Lake is a winding, idyllic stream (serpentine) that flows behind the Pagodenburg. Next to the palace on the garden side is the Large Parterre in the simplified form of a Baroque garden with lawns edged with flowerbeds. – The focal point of the view ("point de vue") from the palace is the Cascade (see page 62 to 65).

## LARGE PARTERRE

On the paths bordering the parterre, statues of gods and vases in white Sterzing marble (1769 ff.).

At the corners, marble vases decorated with putti by Roman Anton Boos, 1788 – 1798. – Figures along the central path: left: Cybele, the earth goddess, with mural crown and spade, by Giovanni Marchori; opposite: Saturn with child, also by Marchiori (both signed OP: JOANNIS MARCHIORI on the plinth). – Left: Jupiter with eagle and thunder-bolt, from a model by Ignaz Günther, 1765; opposite: Juno with peacock and mirror from a model by Johann Baptist Straub, 1765, both completed by Dominikus Auliczek, 1772. – Behind the pool, left: Proserpine with sceptre and the owl Ascalaphus; right: Pluto with Cerberus and fork (later erroneously completed as a trident); both from models by the court sculptor Johann Baptist Straub (1772), completed by Dominikus Auliczek in 1778. – On the southern edge of the parterre (from park to palace): Bacchus with goblet and young satyrs, by Roman Anton Boos, 1782; Venus with Cupid and apple; Mercury with staff and cockerel, both commissioned in 1773 from Ignaz Günther and completed by Roman Anton Boos in 1778. – Along the northern edge of the parterre, from palace to park: Diana with quiver and hound; Apollo with lyre, both by Roman Anton Boos, 1785 (Diana group signed R.A. BOOS on the dog's collar); Ceres with sheaf and sickle, by Roman Anton Boos, 1782. – The two lions on the steps with the Bavarian electoral coat-of-arms by Roman Anton Boos, 1775 (replaced by copies in 1972).

## SOUTH CABINET GARDEN

In the 18th century "little cabinet gardens" – "giardini secreti" –with a north-south axis were laid out next to Zuccalli's buildings with the apartments of the Elector and Electress. In the south garden, which was converted into a landscape garden by Friedrich Ludwig Sckell in the reign of Max Joseph at the beginning of the 19th century, two 18th-century constructions have been preserved: the Small Cascade and the aviary.

*Small Cascade.* This was designed in 1764 by François Cuvilliés the Elder and completed by his son, François Cuvilliés the Younger, in 1768. The classicist architec-

ture surrounding it dates from the early 19th century. In the centre niche there was originally a replica of the famous Venus Italica by Antonio Canova, which is now in the Munich Residence. It has been replaced by a copy of the "Venus of Esquilin" found in Rome in 1874. In the side niches are stone sculptures of Leda with the swan and satyr with the boy Bacchus, both signed Konrad Eberhard, Rome 1810 or 1812. In front of the cascade a group of two

*Baroque marble statue*
*in the palace park*

*South Cabinet Garden with aviary by F. Cuvilliés the Elder, 1751–1757*

figures: Diana hastening towards Endymion. Both signed Konrad Eberhard, Rome 1820 (currently in storage).

*Aviary:* Octagonal building which could originally also be heated. With his love of exotic birds, Max III Joseph commissioned a "canary house" to be built near his apartments. The building, which was begun in 1751, was designed by François Cuvilliés the Elder and probably completed in 1757. The painting on the façade, which has been restored many times (most recently in 1974) is by Ambrosius Hörmannstorfer, who completed the gold leaf work and marbling in the Altes Residenztheater of Munich in 1753. The painting inside the aviary, which was also his work, has been destroyed. As can be seen from the remaining fragments, there were trellises painted in the corner niches. In the middle of the room there was originally a fountain with a round basin. In 1752 the Munich court sculptor Johann Baptist Straub was paid for a lead basin with four shells, which he had completed for the aviary. The building was altered in the early 19th century.

*"Ludwigsgärtchen" with wooden bridge and pavilion*

The ground-floor apartment of Max IV Joseph, who became King Max I, was next to the South Cabinet Garden, which was one of his favourite places. It also contained rare animals and exotic plants, with two black swans swimming in the cascade pool. (The garden is not accessible).

## SUMMERHOUSE IN THE "LUDWIGSGÄRTCHEN"

In around 1800, separate little gardens with summerhouses etc. were laid out near their parents' apartment and adjacent to the South Cabinet Garden, for the children of the electoral family. The largest of these, the "Ludwigsgärtchen" on the path to the Amalienburg, was for the Elector's heir and subsequent crown prince Ludwig. The small, fenced landscape garden has a spring fed from the park canal which bubbles out of a rock, a stream and a pond. The wooden pavilion was originally known as the "Summerhouse of His Highness the Crown Prince".

The main part of the wood-framed building consists of two octagonal rooms one above the other, which are connected by stairs in the projecting part of the building. The upper room has a ceiling curved like the shallow dome of the roof – which is crowned with a half moon – and a gallery projecting from it like a balcony. The boards of the façades are painted to look like stone, and the projecting part of the building painted to look like a brick ruin (it was thus known as the "witch's house"). It is papered inside with hand-printed wallpaper from the year it was built, which has now been restored.

The summerhouse with its two salons was probably used by the whole electoral and subsequently royal family. It was built from 1799 and resembles English summerhouses of the period, particularly with its sliding windows.

Restoration 1980/83. (The summerhouse is not accessible.)


AMALIENBURG

(Text page 67 to 81)


FORMER MENAGERIE

A single-storey building with a mansard roof by the park wall between the Amalienburg and Badenburg. It was built as a pheasantry for Elector Max III Joseph (for golden pheasants), and enlarged under King Max I as a menagerie, to which other buildings in the southern garden area also originally belonged. (Not accessible).

*Landscape garden by the Pagodenburg Lake*

## GROUP OF HOUSES WITH THE "GREEN PUMP HOUSE"

On the way to the Badenburg near the former Menagerie is a group of houses still existing from the 18th century. Picturesque groups of cottages ("hamlets") like this were a favourite embellishment of Baroque gardens. (The complex is not accessible).

The two-storey house in the middle, the "Green Pump House" was built in 1762 and altered in 1803. Before then, instead of the hipped roof there were two high, obelisk-like water towers, which became superfluous when cast iron water pipes were introduced. It contains the pumping equipment designed by Joseph Baader in 1803/1804 and 1817, which still operates the large fountain in the garden parterre. Both machines are masterpieces from the early days of technology. They were completed by Franz Höß, who was in charge of palace fountains. On the west side of the bell-shaped air chamber of the older machine is the following (centred) inscription: MAXIMILIANI IOSEPHI IV /

*Landscape garden by the Badenburg Lake*

ELECTORIS / IVSSV et AVSPICII / construxit / IOSEPHVS BAADER / inventor M D CCC III (1803). – On a measuring instrument on the east side of the machine: Frz: Höss kgl. Hofbrunnen-Meister in München / 1851 (responsible by royal appointment for palace fountains in Munich).

(The second large fountain in the crescent in front of the palace is operated by machinery in the Johannis Tower in the Orangerie. It was designed by Joseph Baader in 1807, and installed by Franz Höß in 1808; the date is recorded on the base. In 1853 it was rebuilt by Höß in cast iron. – It was restored in 1974/75).

Near the group of houses were two pools with hutches for beavers, introduced in 1754 by Max III Joseph. Near the bridge over the canal are locks put in for boats in 1765, also in the reign of Max III Joseph.

## BADENBURG

(Text page 82 to 89)

### PAN STATUE

At the east end of Badenburg Lake, by the path to the Pagodenburg, the figures of Pan playing the flute and a goat were erected by order of King Max I Joseph on a rock placed here for the purpose, with a spring at its base. The marble sculpture was created in 1815 by the court sculptor Peter Lamine. A similar group by Lamine (1774) stands in the palace park of Schwetzingen.

### MONOPTEROS

On a spit of land projecting from the north shore of Badenburg Lake, this building is visible from almost every part of the shore. It was preceded by a round temple made of wood, a copy of the Vesta Temple at Tivoli, with ten Ionic columns and a statue of Apollo in the middle; this building was designed by Friedrich Ludwig Sckell. On 23 February 1862, Leo von Klenze submitted a design commissioned by King Ludwig I for the present Monopteros, which the court builder Carl Mühlthaler did not however complete until 1865. The round temple built of yellow-grey sandstone has painted decoration in the ancient style on the frieze below the cornice and in the coffered dome. The inscription on the stele in the centre of the temple, which is supported by Corinthian columns, translates as follows:

ELECTOR MAXIMILIAN / EMANUEL LAID OUT THIS GARDEN IN THE FRENCH / STYLE IN THE LAST QUARTER / OF THE XVIIth CENTURY, (IT WAS) ALTERED IN THE / ENGLISH STYLE BY / KING MAXIMILIAN JOSEPH / IN THE FIRST (QUARTER) OF THE XIXth. / TO WHOM THIS MEMORIAL (WAS ERECTED) BY / LUDWIG I., KING OF BAVARIA / M D CCC LXV.

*Monopteros by the Badenburg Lake*
*L. v. Klenze and C. Mühlthaler, 1862–1865*

63

*Cascade" in Nymphenburg Park with the figures symbolizing the Danube and the Isar by G. Volpini, 1715–1717*

This was laid out by Joseph Effner in 1717, still in the reign of Max
Emanuel; the marble facing was added in 1796 under Max III Joseph.
The present arrangement of sculptures was only set up in the late 18th
century, some of the figures originating from Schleißheim. The reclin-
ing figures, river god and nymph, symbolizing the Danube and the Isar,
are by Giuseppe Volpini, 1715–1717. The lower pair of figures, also by
Giuseppe Volpini: Minerva with the owl, 1718–21 and Hercules with
the lion, 1722–23 (replaced in 1998 with marble copies by F. Leschinger
and A. Geith), Flora and Aeolus god of the winds, around 1725; by Roman Anton Boos: Mars with sword and shield, Minerva with spear and
shield, both first commissioned from Ignaz Günther – Thetis with dolphin, from a model by Charles de Groff, 1765, completed in 1775, and
Neptune with sea-horse, 1737, by Guillaume de Groff.

## PAGODENBURG – MAGDALENENKLAUSE

(Text pages 90 to 97 and pages 97 to 102)

## THE GLASSHOUSES

North of the Large Parterre, in separate ornamental gardens, are three
glasshouses built for King Max I from plans based on English designs
by Friedrich Ludwig Sckell. They reflect the growing interest in botany
in the early 19th century and the King's love of tropical plants. When
they were built, the Nymphenburg glasshouses were the most modern
in Germany and are for this reason of great historical value. The whole
complex, with the buildings arranged in a line and the ornamental gardens in front, is an excellent example of the simple, monumental style
of classicist art.

*The "Iron House",* the first of the three glasshouses, was completed in 1807. The middle section of this gallery-style building, made primarily of glass and iron, was
originally a wood and glass construction which burned down in 1867. Carl
Mühlthaler rebuilt the plant tract in steel and widened the northern section in the
process; one of the most remarkable features he introduced was the early form of

double glazing. The glasshouse was filled with plants from Japan, China, India, Australia, South America and Africa and in the corner buildings were salons for the King. The arrangement of the various sections and the decoration on the outside etc. make it more than a merely functional building. Above the west portal is the inscription VERE FRVOR SEMPER / FLORAE NITIDISSIMVS HORTUS. (Of veritable enjoyment forever, a luxuriant garden of flowers). Above the east portal: FLORAE AVSTRALI / SACRVM: (Sanctum of flowers of the south). Garden parterre with circular pool and fountain sculpture by Peter Lamine, 1816.

*Glasshouse with a higher middle section* (today the "Geranium House"). Completed in 1816, and still in its original architectural form, it was intended for the growing of young plants. The construction of the "light-filled plant room" is based on Sckell's own experiments and studies. It had a glass front and the ceiling curved away from it describing a quarter circle that reached to the floor "so that more light can be admitted and reflected on the plants". In front of the glasshouse a semicircular ornamental garden with four sandstone figures: the Judgement of Paris (Paris, Venus, Juno, Minerva) by Landolin Ohnmacht, Straßburg, 1804–1807). In the middle a circular pool with a fountain sculpture by Johann Nepomuk Haller from a model by Peter Lamine, 1818.

*"Palm House".* This glasshouse (now renovated and used as a café) was built in 1820 and filled mainly with exotic palms and plants. In 1830 the iron stoves installed by Sckell were replaced by the first hot water heating in Germany. The building was completely renewed in 1965–68, when more windows were installed on the north side and the width of the plant hall was reduced. – In the flower parterre in front a circular pool with a small fountain.


NORTH CABINET GARDEN.

Corresponding to the garden on the southern side, a cabinet garden was also laid out next to the two blocks on the north side of the palace. This little French-style garden was originally surrounded by an arbour with marble busts on square pillars. The sculptures, which are still in place, were probably by the court sculptors of Max Emanuel. (Not accessible).

# THE PAVILIONS

To visit the pavilions Amalienburg, Badenburg, Pagodenburg and Magdalenenklause, in that order, take the shorter route round the park, which follows the longer one as far as the Badenburg. From the Badenburg there is a direct connection via the central canal to the Pagodenburg.

## AMALIENBURG

Built in 1734–1739 during the reign of Karl Albrecht as a little hunting lodge for Electress Maria Amalia. The architect is authenticated as François Cuvilliés the Elder. Single-storey building in the form of a "trianon" with an elongated ground plan, in which the raised central room roofed with a dome is convex on one side, while on the other the curve of the projecting wings suggests a small cour d'honneur (it was originally closed off by a projecting area with a central ramp framed by a strip of lawn). The attic was originally crowned with 16 vases (from a model by Johann Baptist Zimmermann), which were reconstructed in 1991. The exterior decoration is restrained. Over the main portal is a graceful group of figures with the hunting goddess Diana in the centre by Johann Baptist Zimmermann. In the round niches busts of satyrs. Inside, the unique artistic unity of the suite of rooms and the wealth of the decoration combine to produce an interior of exceptional beauty. The stucco-work is by Johann Baptist Zimmermann, the carving by Joachim Dietrich and the delicate decorative painting by Joseph Pascalin Moretti.

The figures over the main portal, almost sculptures in the round, and on the cornice of the central hall, as well as the elegant, courtly figures on the panelling of the bedroom, are more than just decorative art. This fact and the note in the archives that Egidius Verhelst the Elder worked from 1735–39 on the "exquisite buildings" of Nymphenburg,

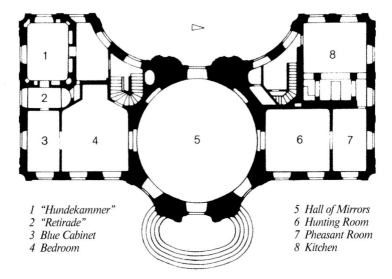

1 "Hundekammer"
2 "Retirade"
3 Blue Cabinet
4 Bedroom

5 Hall of Mirrors
6 Hunting Room
7 Pheasant Room
8 Kitchen

*Ground floor of the Amalienburg*

indicate that Verhelst or his workshop "contributed" to the figures decorating the Amalienburg. The archives record in addition that the Dutch sculptor and "ornamental carver" Wolfgang Jakob Gerstens, who had already been summoned from Holland in the reign of Max Emanuel, completed work "of various kinds" in the Amalienburg. His style can be recognized in the rich carving of the silver console tables in the Hall of Mirrors.

Today the Amalienburg, like the other pavilions, is set in the landscape garden laid out by Friedrich Sckell. On a 1755 plan of Nymphenburg Park, however, it stands in the middle of a bosket in an open area with eight paths bordered with high hedges radiating from it. An avenue of fountains leads to the Amalienburg from the east, with a broad aisle crossing it at right angles. Visitors approaching the Amalienburg did not see the whole building until they reached this point.

*Landscape Garden with the Amalienburg*

The delicate pink and white of the façade corresponds to the original colours of 1736, and was restored on the basis of findings in 1986. While the apparent reversal of the colours between the outer and central projections is consistent with the construction of the walls, it was also designed by Cuvilliés as a special feature that would immediately appeal to visitors as they emerged from the corridors of hedges. The original colours of the interior, which were uncovered during the restoration in 1956/58, correspond to the colour data on the ground-plan of the Amalienburg by François Cuvilliés the Younger of 1771. According to this, the silvered decoration in the Hall of Mirrors was on a white background ("à fond Blanc"), information which evidently refers to the decoration on the cupola which is the dominating feature of the room. For the Bedroom and the Hunting Room two tones of "yellow" are given as the basic colour, straw (fond Couleur de Paille) and lemon ("fond Citron"). – The Amalienburg was first restored as early as 1769 under Max III Joseph, with the court stucco worker Franz Xaver Feichtmayr the Younger as one of the craftsmen.

## 1    "Hundekammer" (Dog room)

Panelled room with recesses for the dogs and cupboards for the guns. The blue Camaieu painting in the "Indian" style by Joseph Pascalin with which the walls and ceilings are decorated imitates the style of Dutch tiles. Between the flowers and fruits of the early Rococo decoration are numerous hunting motifs, including the owl as a decoy bird. Over the doors are roebuck and fox hunts (a dog with the monogramme CA = Carl Albrecht). In the window-jambs lightly painted landscapes with motifs from the Nymphenburg hunting grounds have been preserved in their original form. – One rounded room corner is faced with tiles which conceal a stove.

## 2    "Retirade"

Panelling with blue-and-white decoration, and between the panels still-lifes of flowers with animals by Franz de Hamilton and Arcadian landscapes. The rear wall was used as a commode, with a toilet chair concealed behind its folding doors. In the niche and on the ceiling decorative painting by Joseph Pascalin Moretti.

## 3    Blue Cabinet

South corner room of this magnificent suite of residential rooms. On the dado, door panels and shutters elaborately carved silver ornamentation. Silver stucco-work on the ceiling and beautifully carved hunting trophies on the wings of the door to the bedroom.

*Furnishings:* 4 taborets and Venetian glass chandelier from the time the Amalienburg was built.

Light blue damask wall covering last renewed in 1990, as were also the curtains.


## 4   Bedroom

The walls are richly decorated in silver and yellow ("fond Citron"). The hunting theme of the carvings on the panelled walls – one of the most exquisite examples of Rococo decoration – is continued without interruption in the stucco-work decoration of the ceiling. The carved figures on the rear wall of the bed alcove are exceptionally beautiful. On either side of the bed alcove are portraits of Elector Prince Albrecht and Maria Amalia in hunting dress from the atelier of George Desmarées.

*Furnishings:* Commode-shaped console table (Joachim Dietrich from a design by François Cuvilliés the Elder). Here and in the following rooms, Venetian chandeliers belonging to the original décor.

Originally there was a clock with a pagod on the mantelpiece (with the name of Gudin le jeune on the mechanism) and candelabra with Fo dogs in "blanc de chine" on silver-bronze stands (inventory of 1763, currently in storage).

Daybed ("lit en niche") and curtains reconstructed in 1991 in slightly simplified form, based on the inventory description of 1758.


## 5   Hall of Mirrors

With its unique silver decoration this hall, which is circular with a flat cupola, is the most beautiful room in the palace. Where previously rooms were structured with classical forms (pilasters, columns, pillars), these are now replaced by rocaille decoration. The walls are a succession of windows and mirrors, admitting the world of the garden outside into the interior. The themes of the ceiling stucco-work with the four figures of Diana, Amphitrite, Ceres and Bacchus are hunting and the pleasures of the table. The room was used for banquets, balls, concerts and relaxation after the hunt.

*Furnishings:* Console tables set in silver with rich shell ornamentation (rocailles) and elaborately carved silvered stools.

*Detail of the magnificent carving on the  wall panelling of the"Retirade"*
*in the Amalienburg (Room 4)*

*"Retirade" in the Amalienburg (Room 4)*
*with a portrait of Elector Karl Albrecht*

73

*Detail of the lavish stucco-work in the Amalienburg's*
*Hall of Mirrors (Room 5)*

*Hall of Mirrors in the Amalienburg (Room 5)*

## 6 Hunting Room

The walls are decorated in silver and yellow ("couleur de Paille"). Wall paintings with festival and hunting themes by Peter Jakob Horemans in stucco frames, animals in the style of Franz de Hamilton and two Seine landscapes (St. Cloud near Paris and Meudon) by Jean Baptiste Feret.

The room, which could be heated by an open fire, is designed as a small gallery, with the paintings arranged above one another in the 18th century fashion.

*List of paintings, from left to right:*

BOTTOM ROW:

*Fireplace wall:* Seine landscape near Meudon. – Seine landscape near St Cloud with the palace parterre in the foreground. Both painted by Jean Baptiste Feret, 1712, in memory of Elector Max Emanuel's exile. Originally in the small gallery of the first north block in the main palace.

*Hunting Room in the Amalienburg (Room 6),*
*a miniature art gallery*

*Exit wall (to the north):* River landscape with wild animals. – River landscape with birds. Both paintings in the style of Franz de Hamilton.

*Entrance wall (to the south):* River landscape with a variety of birds. – Hilly landscape with stags and hares. Both in the style of Franz de Hamilton.

TOP ROW:

The top row of paintings is a series of six illustrations of court festivals and hunting from the reign of Elector Karl Albrecht, for whom the Amalienburg was built. They are some of the first works commissioned by the Elector from Peter Jakob Horemans (1700–1775) of Antwerp. Five of the paintings were specially painted for the Amalienburg when it was built from 1734–1739. The sixth –Falconry by the Vogelhaus – was added shortly after 1770. According to Horemans himself, the six paintings "in Amalienburg [contain] over 200 portraits".

FIREPLACE WALL:

*Round races at the Elector's court at Fürstenried Palace.*

This was painted in 1732. The event depicted was part of the festivities marking the birth of the heir Maximilian Joseph and the beginning of the reign of Karl Albrecht in the spring of 1727. "On 14 May at the Electoral summer residence and hunting lodge of Fürstenried a country wedding was held by their Highnesses the Electoral family and members of the high nobility, followed by a tournament held by her Highness the Electress and her Highness the Duchess [Maria Anna] and other ladies, in fine new carriages specially made for the occasion. Both their Highnesses were driven by their Highnesses the Elector and Duke Ferdinand, the others by the cavaliers, and the Electress won the contest with the lance."

In the carriage drawn by two horses in the foreground is Electress Maria Amalia, driven by Elector Karl Albrecht. A Cavalier bears a pole, on which is the head of a Turk as a trophy. – On the left next to them is Duke Ferdinand Maria and Maria Anna of Bavaria. – In the background festive architecture in the form of a triumphal arch, and completing the picture Fürstenried Palace. – The women dressed as "Roman ladies" for the round race. Steered round the race course by cavaliers, they had to hit the heart of a cupid with lances and darts, wound a chicken that lay in the mouth of a fox with a dagger, and hit the shield of a figure with a ball. The winners were rewarded with various prizes.

*Tournament races on stags near Allach at the "Green House".*

Painted in 1734. Festivities on 15 May 1727: "On 15 May, when the esteemed magistrate and citizenry of the residency of Munich came to pay homage, a tournament on live animals was held between two small woods between Nymphenburg, Allach and Mosen ... whereby His Highness the Elector had the best results in the dagger and pour la Dame contests; His Highness Duke Ferdinand won the arrow contest, and His Highness Duke Theodor the lance contest."

The rider on the stallion in the foreground is possibly Johann Theodor, Prince-Bishop of Freising etc. – At the tournament red and fallow deer were driven into elongated enclosures and brought down as the riders went by with lances, darts, daggers and pistols. – In the background, as in the previous picture, festive architecture in the form of triumphal arches. The "Green House" was one of the electoral hunting lodges between Moosach and Untermenzing.

EXIT WALL (TO THE NORTH):

*Riding to the hounds under Elector Karl Albrecht at the "Yellow House".*

Painted in 1736. Riding to the hounds at the "Yellow House", near Fürstenried Palace. In the middle Elector Karl Albrecht on the light-coloured horse. To the right of him Elector Clemens August of Cologne. On the left probably Ferdinand Maria and Johann Theodor, the other brothers. – In the background the "Yellow House" a little hunting lodge built in the form of a miniature palace, and described by the Bamberg architect J.M. Küchel as follows: "This yellow house has 4 sections, with rooms in 3 of them and the stairs in the 4th, and in the middle an octagonal hall; upstairs are 6 rooms. The whole building is of wood and all the rooms are wallpapered, every one in a different paper, and from every window there is a view of an avenue, which is at least an hour's journey long; in all, this little building is very pretty ... "

*Elector Karl Albrecht changes his boots at the "Blue House" after a fall.*

Painted in 1738. The incident took place on 26 November 1734 in the Forstenrieder Park. The Elector fell off his horse and into the water while pursuing a wild boar over the River Würm. He took off his heavy riding boots to wade across the river and rode barefoot to the "Blue House", where he put on dry boots and clothing. In the centre of the picture the Elector with servants. Also depicted are Duke Johann Theodor and the seven-year-old electoral heir Max Joseph. In the middle distance to the right Electress Maria Amalie is getting into a coach and next to her is Elector Clemens August of Cologne, also changing his boots. – The "Blue House" was around an hour south of Maria Eich near Planegg.

*Elector Karl Albrecht and Electress Maria Amalia with courtiers engaged in falconry at the "Vogelhaus".*

Painted after 1741. The hunt in question took place on 29 June 1741. In the centre of the group is Elector Karl Albrecht, to the right of him the Electress, behind her Duke Ferdinand Maria. Left of Karl Albrecht is his heir Max Joseph, still further left, with a light-coloured falcon on his hand, Elector Clemens August of Cologne. The aviary was one of the permanent hunting buildings, and was located, judging by the silhouette of Munich in the background, near Nymphenburg Palace.

*Elector Karl Albrecht at a "German hunt" by the "Red House".*

Painted in 1739. "German hunting" involved the pursuit on horseback of bears or fierce wild boars The animals were caught by the dogs and then killed by the hunter.

In the centre of the picture Karl Albrecht on horseback, about to kill the boar captured by the dogs with his dagger. The Elector is surrounded by members of his family. Behind a riding group to the right is the Electress in a coach. The "Red House" was located southwest of Pasing on the River Würm.

*Window pillar:* Four paintings one above the other: hunting animals and game.

*Furnishings:* Commode: Wolfgang Jakob Gerstens from a design by François Cuvilliés the Elder.

Silvered taborets covered in brocade interwoven with silver thread, from the original furnishings.

Above the fireplace a valuable wall clock by the Parisian clockmaker C. P. G. Mesnil made of Chinese porcelain from the K'ang –hsi period with Meissen flowers (at present in storage).


## 7    Pheasant Room or "Indian Cabinet"

Counterpart of the Blue Cabinet. The large wooden panels on the walls, covered with coarse, glue-primed linen, are decorated with ornamental painting interspersed with pheasants on a light-blue background, in imitation of Chinese wall coverings. The motifs were origi-

*Kitchen of the Amalienburg (Room 8), the walls decorated
with brightly-coloured Dutch tiles*

nally outlined in gold and silver, of which. only fragments remain, and the colours have largely faded.

As the writing cabinet of Maria Amalia, which had a lacquered "pearl-coloured" writing table with silver fittings, this, the smallest room in the building, was originally the most colourful of them all. – On the ceiling silvered stucco-work.

## 8   Kitchen

The lavish artistic decoration makes this kitchen quite unique. The walls are covered with blue-and white and coloured Dutch tiles, the coloured tiles assembled to form pictures of magnificent vases of flowers and everyday life in China in the style of Chinese vase painting. The ceiling and wooden panelling is painted with blue chinoiseries on a white background, the work of Joseph Pascalin Moretti.

The tiles forming the three multicoloured flower vase pictures are probably from the "Rose" manufactory in Delft. The motif is almost identical with four multicoloured floor vases from the same manufactory in a ground-floor room in Rambouillet Palace in France. The Rambouillet room was created in 1715–1730 and covered completely with Dutch tiles; it was probably used by the Comtesse de Toulouse as a dining room. In the Amalienburg some of the tiles forming the rare coloured pictures of Chinese scenes have been put in the wrong place. The blue-and-white tiles have the usual Biblical, mythological and landscape motifs. – The walls are given additional structure with tiles painted with a manganese-coloured motif of twisted, garlanded, pillars.

The magnificent decoration of this room, adjacent to the private writing cabinet of the Electress rather than in the cellar or the subsidiary building that once stood on the south side of the Amalienburg, probably derives from the fact that "the late Electress herself used to cook", as the children Nannerl and Wolfgang Amadeus Mozart were told when they visited the Amalienburg in 1763.

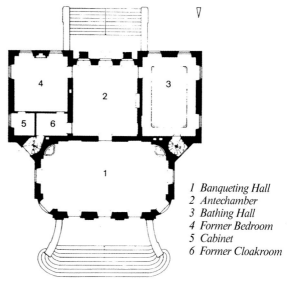

1 Banqueting Hall
2 Antechamber
3 Bathing Hall
4 Former Bedroom
5 Cabinet
6 Former Cloakroom

*Ground floor of the Badenburg*

## BADENBURG

The Badenburg, unique of its kind, is located in the south part of the park opposite the Pagodenburg, which was used as a teahouse. It was built as a little bathing palace in 1718–21 by Joseph Effner for Elector Max Emanuel, probably inspired at least in part by the Turkish bathhouses the Elector had seen as imperial commander during the fighting in Hungary in around 1685/86. The ground-plan of the two-storey building is dominated by the large reception and banqueting hall, which projects from the rest of the building. The small adjacent apartment to the south contains the splendid Bathing Hall, which is carried through two floors (the basement and the ground floor). The main façade of the garden building was originally decorated with stuccowork by the French sculptor and stucco-worker Charles Dubut; the at-

*View of the Badenburg from the northeast*

tic was crowned with lead vases. In the early 19th century the façade was altered in accordance with the classicist style of the time by Leo von Klenze and the stucco-work was removed. In front of the little bathing palace, as part of the geometric garden and as an approach to the building, Effner had laid out a terrace with a large pool and numerous fountains, while the south side had a flower parterre. The setting of the Badenburg was altered completely by Friedrich von Sckell, who transformed the bosket garden into a landscape garden with the creation of a "natural" lake and the "Löwental", lion valley (named after the two lions by Charles de Groff, made in 1769 for the south steps of the Badenburg), and the building itself became "staffage".

After the bomb damage from the last war had been repaired, the Badenburg underwent thorough restoration from 1975/80. The ceiling picture in the hall by Jacopo Amigoni was almost completely destroyed, with only fragments of the figures at its edges remaining. The restoration by Karl Manninger (1984) was based on the colours established from the remaining fragments and prewar colour photos. The chance finding of the old wallpaper of the Antechamber also aided in the decoration of the little palace; after its restoration the paper was put up in its original room, replacing a silk covering dating from the 19th century. – All the wallpaper in the Badenburg rooms was restored between 1985 and 1988, and mounted on special frames covered in canvas.

## 1    Banqueting Hall

The hall is two storeys high and dominated by round-arched glass doors with oval windows above them. The white stucco-work, in the sumptuous forms of the late Baroque era, is by Charles Dubut. There is a predominance of flowers, fruits and naturalistic seashells, illustrating the themes of gardens and water. Filling the scotia in the corners of the room are relief figures symbolizing the elements. The ceiling painting with its abundant figures (almost completely repainted after war damage in 1952/53 and again in 1984) is by Jacopo Amigoni, the only one in Nymphenburg by this Italian artist, who primarily worked on the ceilings in Schleißheim Palace. The depiction of Apollo in his sun chariot dispelling the shades of night is an allegory of morning. The group of bathing nymphs is another reference to the purpose of the little palace. There are also figures symbolizing the four elements fire, water, earth and air. In the corner niches wall fountains with Triton children on dolphins, G. de Groff, 1722.

*Fountain figure*
*by G. de Groff, 1722*

84

*The light-filled Banqueting Hall of the Badenburg (Room 1)*

The red and white marble floor in the hall was reconstructed and the natural oak of the doors, windows and wooden panels was uncovered.

## 2 Antechamber and Games Room

The walls are covered with Chinese wallpaper with sprays of blossom, flowers, exotic birds and butterflies. The reintroduction of this old printed paper, in colour with silver outlines and backed with canvas (probably East-Asian work commissioned from Europe in around 1780/90), has recreated the special atmosphere of this charming 18th-century palace room decorated in the style of the time. The wood was painted white in 1722. Above the fireplace there was originally a beautiful painting by Sebastien Bourdon depicting the release of Andromeda from the rock to which she was chained. This was taken to the Hofgarten Gallery in Munich in 1791 and now hangs in the Alte Pinakothek. Today in its place there is a picture of a rare white fox, shot in the electoral hunting revier of Kling on 9.10.1777, painted by Joseph Stephan.

The stone floor replaces a parquet floor from around 1780.

## 3 Bathing Hall

The magnificent Bathing Hall is unusually large for its time. The bath itself is in the basement, and the lower part was originally faced with lead. The walls above water-level are decorated with blue-and-white "Dutch" tiles. Stucco consoles in the shape of busts, the lower part of which has been restored, support the gallery surrounding the upper section of the room. The magnificent marbled stucco with a reddish background and black panels decorated with agate-coloured relief sections that covers the gallery walls is by the Bavarian stucco-worker Johann Georg Bader. The stuccowork in the scotias was renovated by Johann Baptist Zimmermann as early as 1736. In the wrought-iron railing by the court metalworker Antoine Motté is the monogramme of Max Emanuel (ME), for whom the Badenburg was built, and the electoral crown. The decorative, delicately-tinted ceiling painting (oil on canvas, cleaned and restored in 1952), is by the French artist Nicolas Bertin. It was made in Paris and rolled up for transportation to Munich.

*Magnificent Bathing Hall in the Badenburg (Room 3),*
*the lower part decorated with Dutch tiles*

87

The painting (a grisaille) depicts fountains and mythological scenes re-
volving around the theme of bathing: Hercules hurling a rock at the
water nymphs; Diana bathing; Leda with the swan; Europa swimming
the Hellespont on the Bull.

The bath was entered by a small staircase with tiled walls. The heating system in the basement with a walled-in stove and twisted pipes in
the pool is still in place. The basement rooms included two small
bathing apartments each with a bath-tub and a quiet room as well as a
kitchen with an open fireplace (not accessible).

## 4    Former Bedroom

Chinese wallpaper with "life-sized Indian figures", first mentioned in
the inventory of 1769: hunting party of a high official of the Chinese
emperor. The hand-coloured Chinese wallpaper from the 17th century
– woodcut scenes with small figures – that was discovered underneath
this is now in room 6. The mirror over the fireplace has a richly carved
gilt frame by Johann Adam Pichler with Neptune masks spouting water, mythological beasts and seashells. The bath in the basement was
directly accessible from this former bedroom via a winding staircase.

## 5    Cabinet

Chinese wallpaper painted with small figures in idealized scenes from
everyday life in China (2nd half of the 18th century, acquired from the
art trade in 1954). Ceiling with grotesques and apes as allegories of sci-
ence and astronomy.(Currently closed for restoration).

## 6    Former Cloakroom

The wall covering has been replaced by the original hand-printed wallpaper that was discovered under the present wallpaper in the bedroom.
It was made in China in the early 17th century, and additionally deco-

rated along the joins when first installed in the Badenburg. The woodcuts themselves are so-called New Year pictures, which were produced in China to celebrate the New Year, and include illustrations of scenes from famous Chinese plays and operas or mythology.

On the upper floor of the Badenburg there was a small, simply furnished room for the Elector and the most important members of his retinue. It was partially restored after the destruction in the Second World War (not accessible).

*Woodcut from the "Chinese wallpaper" in*
*the Former Cloakroom of the Badenburg*
*(Room 6)*

*View of the Pagodenburg from the southeast*

## PAGODENBURG

The architect of the elegant, two-storey building constructed in 1716–19 was Joseph Effner. According to tradition, however, the imaginative ground-plan, an octagon with an eight-metre diameter extended with cruciform arms, was the work of Max Emanuel himself. This outline is probably based on French models, such as the "Pavillon du soleil" in Marly, and more especially the octagonal hunting lodge built for Max Emanuel in Bouchefort near Brussels by Germain Boffrand. It also however bears an interesting resemblance to a Turkish seraglio, a building familiar to Europeans from engravings. While the exterior has little to do with Asian art, in the rich decoration of the interior Turkish and Far-Eastern motifs blend seamlessly to create the exotic atmosphere that had just become fashionable but rarely succeeded as it does here. The name of this little palace is said to have originated from its painted decoration "with Chinese figures like pagods (idols)".

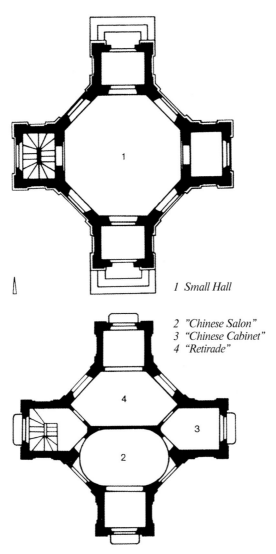

1  Small Hall

2  "Chinese Salon"
3  "Chinese Cabinet"
4  "Retirade"

*Ground floor and upper floor of the Pagodenburg*

Pilasters with Corinthian capitals dominate the exterior – an unusual motif for such a delicate "maison de plaisance". The decorations on the windows and balcony are mainly Rococo versions of the original motifs, produced during a general renovation under François Cuvilliés the Elder in around 1767/68. The present pale grey, beige and white colour scheme also goes back to this time. The surfaces of the attic wall concealing the flat, tented roof were originally decorated with ornamental painting and there were balustrades and ornamental vases on top, which gave the building a more whimsical character. The balconies in French wrought-iron technique are by Antoine Motté, with "fleurons de bronze" by Guillaume de Groff. Over the entrance and the windows of the lower floors are sculptured masks representing Bacchus, Flora, Neptune and Ceres.

The little garden pavilion was used for exclusive parties where the strict formalities of court ceremonies could be relaxed, and in particular as a place to rest from the exertions of playing "mail", a game akin to bowls for which a horse-shoe shaped alley had been created on the north side of the Pagodenburg (today Pagodenburg Valley).

The building was reproduced in the Baden Residence Rastatt: Marchioness Sibylla Augusta sent for copies of the plans from Munich in 1772 and built her own "Pagodenburg", although with a different roof.

In 1961/63 the "Saletl" was restored and the paint covering the scotias since the 19th century was removed. The stucco decoration here was produced using the "combined technique": part of the decoration was applied directly and part made in the workshop and applied in completed form. The original glazed blue and silver of the surrounding panels was uncovered. Numerous restoration measures have been implemented inside and out since this time.

## 1    Ground Floor with Hall and Staircase

On the ground-floor the rooms are arranged in accordance with the ground-plan, with four cabinet-like, rectangular side rooms extending the octagonal central room, the "Saletl". Round the edges of the ornamental ceiling painting in the central room (Johann Anton Gumpp 1718/19) are the Four Continents and busts of mythological figures on

*The Small Hall
on the ground floor
of the Pagodenburg
(Room 1)*

pedestals. The ceiling painting of the entrance room pays homage to Bacchus, that of the cabinet opposite to Venus, and the ceiling in the cabinet on the east side has Bacchanalian scenes on a gold background. The paintings here and on the ceilings of the upper floors are almost all probably true copies made after 1870. As in the upper cabinets, the scotias with stucco strapwork and latticework were evidently from the workshop of Guillaume de Groff, which is documented as having completed the stucco-work in the "Cabinet next to the bowling alley". In the absence of porcelain from Eastern Asia, and with European porcelain in its early days, Max Emanuel selected Dutch faience tiles for the walls of the ground floor and the stair well, to create an exotic, Chinese atmosphere.

The almost 2000 beautifully painted Dutch tiles are decorated with a variety of landscapes and figures and are probably from Rotterdam. On the upper floor are two tile paintings depicting a French garden. The arrangement is reminiscent of the above-mentioned tiled ground-floor room in Rambouillet Palace (cf. Amalienburg kitchen), which has two blue-and-white tile paintings of Amsterdam and Rotterdam by the Rotterdam faïence painter Cornelis Boumeester. The matching blue-and-white tiles on the walls are from a Rotterdam manufactory.

Not only the tile paintings but also the ceiling painting, the stucco on the walls, the tiled boiseries and the furniture are in blue and white, to underline the Far-Eastern character of the interior.

*Paintings:* Two landscape paintings by Pieter Rysbraeck (1655–1729).

*Furnishings:* The present furnishings date from the renovation period under Elector Max III Joseph.

Large round table with a carved stand and 4 sofas in Delft blue and white, around 1770.

Eight-armed carved chandelier, painted blue and white to look like porcelain, by Johann Thomas Sailler, 1762.

## *2–4    Upper Floor*

The clever arrangement of the rooms on the upper floor comes as a surprise, and lends the building additional charm. Two of the cabinets ("Chinese Salon", Room 2; "Chinese Cabinet", Room 3) have interiors in the Eastern-Asian style, with black-and-red lacquering and panels set into it with silk wall coverings which were later replaced by Chinese wallpaper decorated with colourful ornamental flowers and birds. This was probably purchased by Max Emanuel in Paris. The frame system was based on the structure of Chinese screens. The frequently restored ceiling paintings with the "pagods" go back to Johann Anton Gumpp. The furnishings were completed with high-quality furniture from Paris with Japanese lacquer panels: the two lacquer cabinets date from around 1715. Only the third room ("Retirade", Room 4) has gold-and-white Régence panelling. The alcove walls are covered in very rare red-and-green Genoese silk brocade. The two couches and seating, which were part of the original furnishings, are covered in the same material.

Other furniture: Ebony games table with an inlaid chess board, around 1700.

*The "Chinese Salon" on the upper floor of the Pagodenburg (Room 2)*

95

*"Chinese Cabinet" on the upper floor of the Pagodenburg (Room 3)*

*The Magdalenenklause in winter*

## MAGDALENENKLAUSE

The Hermitage, the exterior designed to look like a ruin and the interior a grotto with four adjoining, simple, cell-like rooms, was built by Joseph Effner towards the end of Max Emanuel's reign (from 1725). It is an example of a rather strange type of building that was found in palace gardens in the late 17th and 18th centuries and expressed the idea of escape from court ceremony into solitude for religious and philosophical meditation, the enjoyment of simplicity and the peaceful appreciation of nature. With their consciously designed ruins, "whose appearance indicates poverty", these buildings imitate the half-ruined huts of hermits. The Magdalenenklause is the court counterpart of the hermitages frequently built in monasteries from the 17th century on. Another interesting feature here is the use at this early stage of historicizing (Romanesque, Gothic and Moorish) architectural details.

In accordance with the building's purpose as a place for prayer and monastic living, the rectangular, single-storey building is divided into a chapel and four adjoining residential rooms; there are two apses opposite one another on the short sides (one for the altar and one the bed alcove), and on two of the corners are low rounded oriels. The altar apsis is decorated with Moorish-style windows. Above the entrance on the east side is a Baroque gable, which is designed in the Italian style as an open belfry.

The building originally looked much more like a ruin, as the walls were higher in places, but the roof was almost all lower. In 1750, because of frequent complaints that it let in the water, Max III Joseph had the building covered with the present hipped roof, from which the lantern of the chapel vault scarcely projects.

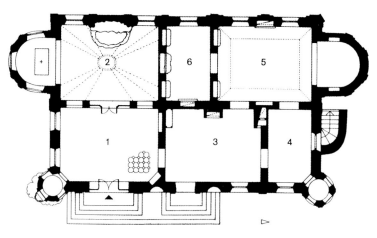

1   Vestibule or
    Grotto Hall
2   Grotto Chapel St Mary
    Magdalene

3   Anteroom
4   Cabinet (library)
5   Refectory
6   Oratory

*Ground plan of the Magdalenenklause*

*Altar niche in the Chapel of the Magdalenenklause,
the walls decorated with grotto work*

Over the entrance, with a wrought-iron barrier across it byAntoine Motté (1726) is a marble slab with an inscription recording the consecration of the chapel by the Archbishop and Elector of Cologne, Clemens August, on 4 April, 1728.

"Among the many monuments of traditional piety left by His Highness the Elector Maximilian Emanuel, this chapel, of which he laid the foundation stone, is the last, and the first of his son, His Highness Elector Carl Albrecht, who completed and decorated it at the beginning of his reign. His Reverend Highness Archbishop and Elector of Cologne, Clemens August, fulfilled his first function as a bishop, in that, with the special permission of his Reverend Highness Prince Johann Theodor, Bishop of Freising and his spiritual administrators, he dedicated the chapel with the usual ceremonies to God the Highest and the Greatest and to the memory of St Mary Magdalene, on White Sunday, 4 April 1728. Present were His Highness Elector Carl Albert, Her Highness Electress Maria Amalia, His Highness Prince Ferdinand Maria and Her Highness his wife Maria Anna Carolina and the Reverend Prince Johann Theodor, Bishop of Freising and Regensburg. In the altar were deposited relics from St Macarius, martyr, St Marianus, martyr, St Maurus, martyr, St Antonia, martyr, St Valentinus, Bishop and St Maurentius, Confessor. The anniversary of the chapel's dedication will be celebrated every year by order of His Reverend Highness and Elector of Cologne, on the 2nd Sunday after Easter.

## 1 + 2  Chapel and Vestibule

The chapel takes up almost half the building. It is divided by two pillars into an anteroom and the chapel proper (Room 2). Both rooms are designed as a grotto: the walls are faced with tuff with artificial coral sprouting from it, and with grotto work (stucco-work with shells, coloured pebbles, stucco birds etc.) The grotto work was completed by Johann Bernhard Joch from Munich in 1726. As the fragments of paint show, it was all once very colourful. The wrought-ironwork at the entrance to the chapel is by the French metalworker Antoine Motté. – In the round room at the outer corner of the anteroom a well shaft was uncovered in 1975, from which a fountain basin outside can also be fed.

The chapel ceiling is a trough vault with coloured stones set like a mosaic and ceiling pictures by Nikolaus Gottfried Stuber with scenes from the life of the repentant Mary Magdalene. The dome opens in a round lantern, which is also encrusted with coloured grotto stones. On the outer wall opposite the entrance is a grotto niche with a stucco figure of St Mary Magdalene by Guiseppe Volpini, 1726. Beneath it is a basin of natural rock with water popularly believed to have healing properties for eyes, but which is in fact diverted from the nearby park canal running at a higher level. The wooden altar, which significantly faces not the entrance but the Elector's rooms, has an antependium inlaid in walnut and maple by the Nymphenburg court woodworker Johann Michael Höcker. The crucifix and candelabra, in keeping with the character of the hermitage, are made rather unusually of narwhale tusk. The two boxwood reliefs are inscribed ›Ignatius Hyllebrand, Bildhauer (sculptor) in Türkheim 1760‹.

## 3–6    Residential rooms

The four rooms – anteroom, cabinet, refectory with alcoves and oratory (Rooms 3 to 6)– are uniformly panelled in simple stained oak with profiled centre sections. The original heating system is still in place with a tiled stove which heats three rooms at once and with everything concealed behind the panelling of the anteroom. The tiles are a different colour in every room (blue, black, green) and decorated with different motifs.

In the former bed alcove, which balances the chapel apse opposite, a Byzantine cross and carved olive-wood chandelier. In the dado below the window facing the chapel in the last room is a prie-dieu, so that Max Emanuel could watch the service from here. The plain wooden furniture is part of the original furnishings, as are also the oil paintings (George Desmarées, St Karl Borromeus, 1739. Repentant Mary Magdalene, Italy, 17th century), the drawings (8 pen and ink drawings of the Passion of Christ by Christoph Schwarz, from 1589), the engravings (including a hermit series by the Sadelers) and the symbolic representations of the Four Last Things, modelled in wax (first half of the 18th century). In the 18th century the majolica dinner service of Duke Albrecht V. (Faenza, Don Pino, 1576) was used here (today in the Munich Residence Museum). According to the old palace inventories, the service with the coat of arms of the Bavarian dukes was kept in large cupboards in the cellar of the Magdalenenklause, where there was also a kitchen. – In the glass cases Chinese and Japanese porcelain, 17th/18th century (K'ang-hsi and Old Imari).

*"Death", from a series of wax reliefs representing the "Four Last Things" in the Madalenenklause*

ELECTOR FERDINAND MARIA, reigned 1651–1679
  Married 1652 to Adelaide (Adelheid Henriette Maria), daughter of
  Duke Victor Amadeus I of Savoy
ELECTOR MAXIMILIAN II EMANUEL, reigned 1679–1726
  First marriage 1685 to Maria Antonia, daughter of Emperor
  Leopold I
  Second marriage 1695 to Therese Kunigunde, daughter of King Johann III Sobieski of Poland
ELECTOR KARL ALBRECHT, reigned 1726–1745, crowned EMPEROR
  KARL VII, 1742
  Married 1772 to Maria Amalia Josepha, daughter of Emperor
  Joseph I.
ELECTOR MAXIMILIAN III JOSEPH, reigned 1745–1777
  Married 1747 to Maria Anna Sophie, daughter of King Friedrich
  August III of Poland and Elector of Saxony
ELECTOR KARL THEODOR, reigned in the Electorate of the Palatinate
  from 1743 and in Palatinate-Bavaria 1777–1799
  First marriage 1742 to Elisabeth Maria Auguste, daughter of the
  Sulzbach Prince Joseph Karl Emanuel
  Second marriage 1795 to Maria Leopoldine, daughter of Archduke
  Ferdinand of Austria-Este
ELECTOR MAX IV JOSEPH (from the Zweibrücken-Birkenfeld line),
  reigned from 1799 as Elector and as KING MAX I JOSEPH 1806–1825
  First marriage 1785 to Auguste Wilhelmine Maria, daughter of
  Landgrave Georg Wilhelm of Hessen-Darmstadt
  Second marriage 1797 to Karoline Friederike Wilhelmine, daughter
  of Prince Karl Ludwig of Baden
KING LUDWIG I, reigned 1825–1848
  Married 1810 to Therese Charlotte Louise, daughter of Duke
  Friedrich of Sachsen-Hildburghausen
KING MAXIMILIAN II JOSEPH, reigned 1848–1864
  Married 1842 to Marie Friederike, daughter of Prince Wilhelm of
  Prussia

KING LUDWIG II, reigned 1864–1886

PRINCE REGENT LUITPOLD, reigned 1886–1912 (third eldest son of King Ludwig I)
Married 1844 to Auguste, daughter of Grand Duke Leopold II of Tuscany

KING LUDWIG III, reigned as Prince Regent 1912–1913 and as King 1913–1918
Married 1868 to Maria Therese, daughter of Archduke Ferdinand of Austria-Este

1663 Kemnath Farm bought for 10,000 florins by Elector Ferdinand Maria for the purpose of building a country residence.

1664 Central section commenced.

1669/95 Mythological ceiling paintings completed by A. Triva in the main palace section.

1671 First garden behind the palace laid out, with flowerbeds radiating from fountains.

1674 H. Zuccalli takes over supervision of the building project.

1675 Vaulting of the central hall.

1701 H. Zuccalli and A. Viscardi start extending the palace with two residential blocks flanking the central building. – At the same time Carbonet begins work on an extensive Baroque garden with "Dutch" canals.

1704 Suspension of all building work because of the Spanish War of Succession.

*Aerial view of Nymphenburg Palace and Park*

*The southern section of the Nymphenburg Palace crescent*

1715 Consecration of the Palace Chapel in the second north block. D. Girard summoned from Paris to look after the park's fountains ("Brunnenmeister").

1716 Building of the second south block completed (Mundkuchl- und Zergaden-Pavillon).

1716/19 Pagodenburg built by J. Effner. Work on the interior of the main palace. Orangerie building commenced.

1718/21 Badenburg built by J. Effner.

1719 East wing of the southern annex completed (Elector's stables on the ground floor, cavaliers' rooms on the first floor). Adjoining farm built.

1720/22 Furnishing of Max Emanuel's apartments on the first floor of the central building and the first north block. The furnishing of the north Antechamber, the adjoining gallery, Max Emanuel's Red Salon (red Lyons silk wall covering recreated in its original form in 1960/61) and the barrel vaulting of the Antechamber in the north block have all been preserved.

1723/24 Connecting wing (Paßgebäude) built (for the "Paßspiel", a game similar to croquet, and billiards), also the third south building tract, fitted out as a kitchen in 1750.

1725/28 Magdalenenklause built by J. Effner.

1728 Building commences in the crescent in front of the palace ("Rondell") with a house for Court Controller Hieber in the southern section.

1729 Construction of the two crescent buildings next to the palace and the second building in the south section of the crescent for cavaliers.

1730 Canal built on the town side of the palace and avenues bordered with lime trees leading to the palace. – East wing of the northern annex built for nuns from Luxembourg. (This tract was handed over in 1835 to the religious order "Englische Fräulein").

1733 ff. Wall built round the gardens.

1733 ff. North wing of the southern rectangular annex extended to provide new stables.

1734/39 The hunting lodge Amalienburg built by F. Cuvilliés the Elder near the new pheasantry.

1739 Consecration of the Chapel built by Effner (destroyed in the Second World War) in the east wing of the northern annex. The original altarpiece (now in the Alte Pinakothek in Munich) a painting by G. B. Tiepolo of St Clemens, the patron saint of the Chapel's founder Elector Clemens August.

1750 "Former Comedihaus" rebuilt as the "Mundt- und Hofkuchl Gebäude" by J. Gunezrhainer. Electoral farm at Nymphenburg destroyed by lightning and rebuilt.

1755/57 Great Hall in the central building reconstructed by F. Cuvilliés the Elder and J. B. Zimmermann.

1757 Completion of the aviary begun in 1751 in the South Cabinet Garden by F. Cuvilliés the Elder. Orangerie tract with the Hubertus Hall built in the north side wing.

1758 Last building on the crescent completed, and from 1761 used for the Porcelain Manufactory founded by Max III Joseph in Neudeck in der Au in 1747.

*Northern canal
with a view of the
Orangerie building*

1761 Bernardo Bellotto, known as Canaletto, paints the two famous views of Nymphenburg Palace for the Residence in Munich.

1762 Pump house built between Amalienburg and Badenburg to operate the big fountains in the Large Parterre and supply the palace with water. This "Green Pump House" was rebuilt in 1803 for the waterworks designed by J. Baader.

1763/64 Alteration of the two corner cabinets in the central building and further renovation of the interior decoration under the supervision of F. Cuvilliés the Elder.

1764 Cascade and fountain designed by F. Cuvilliés the Elder added to the South Cabinet Garden.

1769 Cascade at the west end of the gardens faced in marble. White marble statues of gods produced by order of the Elector for the Large Parterre.

1777/78 New dining hall ("Green Hall") built for the cavaliers on the floor above the court kitchen.

*Northern section
of the crescent with
Baroque buildings*

1778 Reserve for golden pheasants laid out at the edge of the southern half of the park.

1778 Three groups of putti by D. Auliczek placed near the Badenburg. The groups, designed as symbols of the three builders for Elector Max III Joseph, were placed in front of the palace in the early 19th century (today replaced by copies by J. Enderle, completed in 1918; the originals are in the Orangerie tract).

1791 Golden pheasant reserve enlarged as a menagerie building.

1795 The two galleries widened on the garden side with connecting rooms and small rooms.

1799 ff. Wooden summerhouse with the "Crown Prince Garden" built for Prince Ludwig.

1804/23 F. L. v. Sckell transforms the Baroque garden into an English landscape garden.

1806/08 Rebuilding and redecoration of some of the suites and apartments in the main palace.

*Southern canal looking towards the "water corridor"*

1807/08 The pumps designed by J. Baader for the fountains on the town side are installed in the pump house of the Orangerie.

1807 ff. Building of the first glasshouse north of the Large Parterre and renovation of the Small Parterre in front of it from designs by F. L. von Sckell.

1815/16 P. Lamine's statue of Pan playing the flute, with a goat, is set up in the southern half of the park.

1816 and 1820 Two more glasshouses are built from plans by von Sckell. Sculpture of a putto riding on a dolphin in the fountain of the parterre in front by J. N. Haller, 1818. Four mythological figures (Judgement of Paris) by L. Ohnmacht (1804/07) arranged by von Sckell in front of a semicircle of trees.

Around 1820 Classicist architecture (Venus by Canova and mythological figures by K. Eberhard) is introduced behind the cascade of the South Cabinet Garden, which has been transformed in the English style.

1826 Gable over the central building removed and replaced with a wooden cornice by L. v. Klenze.

1835 Renovation of the large waterworks for the fountains on the town side – still in existence – in the pump house of the northern side annex.

1865 King Ludwig I orders the building of the Monopteros from plans by Klenze to commemorate the Nymphenburg gardens.

1938 Rebuilding of the Orangerie tract, completion of the rear sections of the building.

1944 War damage to the north tract and the Badenburg.

1950 The Marstallmuseum (former court coach-house) is set up in the former electoral stables in the southern annex.

1952/53 Restoration of the Badenburg and the Magdalenenklause.

1953/56 Renovation of the façades of the main building.

1956/58 Renovation of the Amalienburg and

1959/60 of the former apartments of Queen Caroline on the first floor of the first southern block with the room where King Ludwig II was born, the "Maserzimmer" and the Blue Salon (here primarily reproduction of the brocaded silk coverings in their original form).

1966/67 Restoration of the second south Antechamber and furnishing of the three rooms next to the North Gallery.

1970/72 Restoration of the façade of the main buildings in their original colours – grey-green on white – on the basis of remaining traces of paint, the veduttas of Beich (1723) in Nymphenburg and the views by Canaletto (Residence).

1974 ff. Restoration of the marble figures. Renewal of the façades of the Orangerie tract. Renovation of the interior of the northern cavaliers' building (Marstallmuseum).

1985 Completion of the comprehensive renovation and restoration of the Badenburg begun in 1978.

1985/86 Thorough restoration of the Pagodenburg and Amalienburg façades.

1986 Completion of the renovation in the northern cavaliers' building begun in 1974. Rearrangement and extension of the Marstallmuseum and opening of the Nymphenburg Bäuml Porcelain Collection in the same tract.

1987/89 New Baroque-style west and southwest wing built by the Marstallhof with workshops and offices for the Bayerische Schlösserverwaltung.

1989 Completion of the renovation and restoration of the "Prince's Building".

1990/95 Restoration work in the Great Hall of the main palace. General renovation of the two south blocks.

1991 Completion of the restoration work on the Palace Chapel begun in 1987.

1993 ff. Renovation of the park wall.

1996 Commencement of comprehensive restoration of the Pagodenburg.

# ALPHABETICAL LIST OF ARTISTS
## AND CRAFTSMEN

# BIBLIOGRAPHY

Oswald Götz, Die Amalienburg im Nymphenburger Schloßpark; in: Städel Jahrbuch 2, 1922 S. 97–108. – L. Hager und H. Kreisel, Nymphenburg, Schloß, Park und Burgen, Amtlicher Führer, München 1938 ff. – H. Kreisel, Die Kunstschreiner der Schloßeinrichtungen des Kurfürsten Max III. Joseph von Bayern im späten Rokoko; in: Münchner Jahrbuch, N. F. 1938/39, Bd. XIII. – H. Kreisel, Farbiges Nymphenburg, München 1944. – Adalbert Prinz von Bayern, Nymphenburg und seine Bewohner, München 1950. – L. Hager, Instandgesetzte Stuckdecken in Schloß Nymphenburg und ihre Meister; in: Deutsche Kunst- und Denkmalpflege, 1953. – L. Hager, Nymphenburg, Schloß, Park und Burgen, München 1955 (mit ausführlicher Bibliographie). – H. Kreisel, Die Instandsetzung der Amalienburg; in: Deutsche Kunst- und Denkmalpflege, 1960. – Christina Thon, Johann Baptist Zimmermann als Stukkator, Diss. phil. Mainz 1965, Ms. – Peter Volk, Zur Geschichte der Nymphenburger Gartenplastik 1716–1770; in: Münch. Jahrb. d. bild. Kunst. 3. F., Bd. 18, 1967, S. 211–240. – L. Frhr. von Gumppenberg, Die Amalienburg im Park von Nymphenburg; in: Der Deutsche Jäger, 86. Jg., April 1968. – Leonore Berghoff, Emanuele Tesauro und seine Concetti, unter besonderer Berücksichtigung von Schloß Nymphenburg, Diss. phil. München 1971, Ms. – Heidi Bürklin, Franz Joachim Beich (1665–1748). Ein Landschafts- und Schlachtenmaler am Hofe Max Emanuels. München 1971 (= Neue Schriftenreihe des Stadtarchivs München Bd. 56). – Gerhard Hojer, Die Baugeschichte des Schlosses Nymphenburg; in: Fee Schlapper u.a., Schloß Nymphenburg, München 1972, S. 108–116. – Michael Petzet, Entwürfe für Schloß Nymphenburg; in: Zwischen Donau und Alpen, Festschrift N. Lieb, München 1972, S. 202–212. – Peter Vierl, Die Erneuerung der Schloßfassaden von Nymphenburg. Ein Beitrag zur Putz- und Stucktechnik in der Denkmalpflege; in: Maltechnik-Restauro 1972, H. 1, S. 36–39; H. 2, S. 100–104; H. 3, S. 205–210. – P. Vierl, Die Putz- und Anstricherneuerung bei der Fassadeninstandsetzung am Schloß Nymphenburg; in: Deutsche Kunst- und Denkmalpflege 1972, S. 43–48. – Liselotte Andersen, Eine unbekannte Quellenschrift aus der Zeit um 1700; in: Münch. Jahrb. d. bild. Kunst, 3. F. Bd. 24, 1793, S. 175–237. – Gisela Vits, Joseph Effners Palais Preysing. Ein Beitrag zur Münchener Profanarchitektur des Spätbarock, Frankfurt/M. 1973 (= Kieler Kunsthistor. Studien Bd. 5). – P. Vierl, Neue Erkenntnisse zur Baugeschichte des Schlosses Nymphenburg; in: Jahrbuch der Bayerischen Denkmalpflege Bd. 29, 1972–74, S. 97–115. – Johann Georg Prinz von Hohenzollern, Peter Jakob Horemans (1700–1776). Ausstellungskatalog, München 1974. – Kurfürst Max Emanuel. Bayern und Europa um 1700 (Ausstellungskatalog), Bd. 1 u. 2, München 1976. – Elmar D. Schmid, Nymphenburg. Schloß und Garten, Pagodenburg, Badenburg, Magdalenenklause, Amalienburg, München 1979. –

(Ausstellungskatalog) Wittelsbach und Bayern III., Bd. 1 u. 2, München 1980. – (Ausstellungskatalog) Klassizismus in Bayern, Schwaben und Franken, München 1980. – Ulrika Kiby-Ratka, Die Küche der Amalienburg im Schloßgarten von Nymphenburg zu München. Heidelberg 1981. – Elmar D. Schmid, Eine unbekannte Ansicht der Magdalenenklause im Schloßpark zu Nymphenburg; in: Weltkunst Jg. 51, 1981, Nr. 13, S. 1959–1961. – Elmar D. Schmid, Bemerkungen zur Restaurierung der Badenburg im Park von Schloß Nymphenburg; in: Ars Bavarica Bd. 31/32, 1983, S. 89–96. – Friederike Wappenschmidt, »Indianische Tapezereyen« in den Münchner Schlössern des 18. Jahrhunderts; in: Ars Bavarica Bd. 31/32, 1983, S. 97–120 (Restaurierungsbericht von M. Heise S. 121–124). – Sabine Heym, Henrico Zuccalli (um 1642–1724). Der kurbayerische Hofbaumeister, München und Zürich 1984. – Dietrich von Frank, Joseph Effners Pagodenburg. Studien zu einer »maison de plaisance«, München 1985. – Uta Schedler, Roman Anton Boos (1733–1810). Bildhauer zwischen Rokoko und Klassizismus, München und Zürich 1985. – Anna Bauer-Wild, Die erste Bau- und Ausstattungsphase des Schlosses Nymphenburg (1663–1680), München 1986. – Wolfgang Braunfels, François Cuvilliés. Der Baumeister der galanten Architektur des Rokoko, München 1986. – Gesche von Deesen, Die Badenburg im Park von Nymphenburg, München 1986. – Gerhard Hojer, Die Amalienburg. Rokokojuwel im Nymphenburger Schloßpark, München und Zürich 1986. – Elmar D. Schmid u. Sabine Heym, Joseph Effner 1687–1745. Bauten für Kurfürst Max Emanuel. Ausstellungstexte, Dachau 1987. – Ellis Kaut, Der Nymphenburger Park, München 1987 (Bildband). – Hermann Bauer und Bernhard Rupprecht, Corpus der barokken Deckenmalerei in Deutschland, Bd. 3, Teil 2, München 1989. – Dietrich von Frank, Die »maison de plaisance«. Ihre Entwicklung in Frankreich und Rezeption in Deutschland, München 1989. – Horst Mellenthin, François Cuvilliés Amalienburg. Ihr Bezug zur französischen Architekturtheorie, München 1989. – Friederike Wappenschmidt, Chinesische Tapeten für Europa. Vom Rollenbild zur Bildtapete, Berlin 1989. – Ulrika Kiby, Die Exotismen des Kurfürsten Max Emanuel in Nymphenburg, Hildesheim, Zürich, New York 1990. – Nikolenko Lada, Schönheitsgalerien der Wittelsbacher, München 1990. – Hildegard Merzenich, Das Nymphenburger Schloßrondell. Mittelpunkt und Denkmal eines Idealstadt-Konzepts; in: Schönere Heimat Jg. 79, 1990, H. 4, S. 235–240. – Kai Uwe Nielsen, Die Magdalenenklause im Schloßpark zu Nymphenburg, München 1990. – Uta Schedler, Die Statuenzyklen in den Schloßgärten von Schönbrunn und Nymphenburg, Hildesheim, Zürich, New York 1990. – Friederike Wappenschmidt, Der Traum von Arkadien. Leben, Liebe, Licht und Farbe in Europas Lustschlössern, München 1990. – Die Möbel der Residenz München. Hrsg. v. Gerhard Hojer u. Hans Ottomeyer. Bd. 1 bearb. v. Brigitte Langer, München 1995; Bd. 2 bearb. v. Brigitte Langer u. Alexander Herzog von Württemberg, München 1996.

# Bayerische Verwaltung der staatlichen Schlösser, Gärten und Seen

## SEHENSWÜRDIGKEITEN

| | | |
|---|---|---|
| Ansbach | **Residenz der Markgrafen von Ansbach;** Prunkappartements des frühen Rokoko, Sammlung Ansbacher Fayencen und Porzellan, Hofgarten mit Orangerie | Tel. 0981/3186<br>Fax 0981/95840 |
| Aschaffenburg | **Schloß Johannisburg** Gemäldegalerie und Kurfürst-liche Wohnräume, Sammlung von Korkmodellen, Schloß-garten; Städtisches Schloß-museum | Tel. 06021/22417<br>Fax 06021/218921 |
| | **Pompejanum;** Nachbildung eines römischen Hauses und Antikenmuseum | |
| | **Schloß und Park Schönbusch** Klassizistisches Schlößchen in englischem Landschaftsgarten | |
| Bamberg | **Neue Residenz Bamberg** Kaisersaal und barocke Prunkräume, Gemäldegalerie, Rosengarten | Tel. 0951/56351<br>Fax 0951/55923 |
| Bayreuth | **Neues Schloß** Markgrafenresidenz aus der Zeit des »Bayreuther Rokoko« mit Museum Bayreuther Fayencen, Hofgarten mit Oran-gerie | Tel. 0921/75969-0<br>Fax 0921/75969-15 |
| | **Markgräfliches Opernhaus** | |
| Bayreuth/<br>Donndorf | **Schloßpark Fantaisie** Historische Gartenanlage | Tel. 0921/75969-0<br>Fax 0921/75969-15 |

| Bayreuth/ Eremitage | **Altes Schloß Eremitage** Wohnräume der Markgräfin Wilhelmine, Grotte, historische Gartenanlage mit Wasserspielen | Tel. 0921/75969-0 Fax 0921/75969-15 |
| Bayreuth/ Wonsees Sanspareil | **Morgenländischer Bau** Stilräume, Gartenparterre und Felsengarten | Tel. 0921/75969-0 Fax 0921/75969-15 |
| | **Burg Zwernitz,** Burganlage | |
| Burghausen | **Burg zu Burghausen** Burganlage, Stilräume, Gemäldegalerie | Tel. 08677/4659 Fax 08677/65674 |
| Coburg | **Schloß Ehrenburg** Historische Wohn- und Prunkräume des Barock und 19. Jahrhunderts | Tel. 09561/8088-0 Fax 09561/8088-40 |
| Coburg/ Rödental | **Schloß Rosenau** in englischem Landschaftsgarten, Wohnräume der Biedermeierzeit und neugotischer Marmorsaal | Tel. 09563/4747 Fax 09561/8088-40 |
| Dachau | **Schloß Dachau;** Festsaal, historische Gartenanlage | Tel. 08131/87923 Fax 08131/78573 |
| Eichstätt | **Willibaldsburg** Festungsanlage, Juramuseum, Ur- und Frühgeschichtsmuseum, Hortus Eystettensis | Tel. 08421/4730 Fax 08421/8194 |
| Ellingen | **Residenz Ellingen;** Prunkappartements des Fürsten Wrede, Deutschordensräume, Schloßkirche, historische Gartenanlage | Tel. 09141/3327 Fax 09141/72953 |

| | | |
|---|---|---|
| Herrenchiemsee | **Neues Schloß** | Tel. 08051/6887-0 |
| | **Herrenchiemsee** | Fax 08051/6887-99 |
| | Wohn- und Repräsentations- | |
| | räume, historische Gartenan- | |
| | lage mit Wasserspielen und | |
| | **König Ludwig II. Museum** | |
| | | |
| | **Museum im Alten Schloß** | |
| | Dauerausstellung zur ehema- | |
| | ligen Klosteranlage und zum | |
| | Verfassungskonvent; Stilräume | |
| | König Ludwigs II. | |
| | | |
| Höchstädt | **Schloß Höchstädt** | Tel. 08431/8897 |
| | Kapelle mit Sammlung | Fax 08431/42689 |
| | südwestdeutscher Fayencen | |
| | | |
| Kelheim | **Befreiungshalle** | Tel./Fax 09441/1584 |
| | | |
| Kempten | **Residenz Kempten** | Tel. 0831/256-1 |
| | Prunkräume und Thronsaal | und 0831/256-251 |
| | der Fürstäbte | Fax 0831/256-260 |
| | | |
| Königssee | **St. Bartholomä;** Jagdschloß, | Tel. 08652/96360 |
| | Kapelle St. Johann und Paul, | Fax 08652/64721 |
| | Naturpark Berchtesgaden | |
| | | |
| Kulmbach | **Plassenburg;** Schöner Hof, | Tel. 09221/8220-11 |
| | historische Markgrafenzimmer, | Fax 09221/8220-26 |
| | Gemäldegalerie, Jagdwaffen- | |
| | sammlung | |
| | | |
| Landshut | **Stadtresidenz;** Stilräume und | Tel. 0871/92411-0 |
| | Gemäldegalerie, Kreis- und | und 0871/92411-44 |
| | Stadtmuseum | Fax 0871/92411-40 |
| | | |
| | **Burg Trausnitz** | |
| | Burganlage mit Burgkapelle | |
| | St. Georg, Stilräume | |
| | | |
| Lauenstein bei | **Burg Lauenstein** | Tel./Fax 09263/400 |
| Ludwigstadt | Burganlage, Wohnräume, | |
| | volkskundliche Sammlungen | |

| Linderhof | **Schloß Linderhof** | Tel. 08822/9203-0 |
| | Wohn- und Repräsentations- | Fax 08822/9203-11 |
| | räume, Venusgrotte, Marokka- | |
| | nisches Haus, Maurischer Kiosk | |
| | und Hundinghütte, historische | |
| | Gartenanlage mit Wasser- | |
| | spielen | |

München

**Residenzmuseum** — Tel. 089/29067-1
Historische Wohn- und Prunk- Fax 089/29067-225
räume aus der Zeit der Renais-
sance bis zum 19. Jahrhundert,
Hofkirchen und -kapellen, Spe-
zialsammlungen (Silber, Porzellan, Paramente, Reliquien)

**Schatzkammer**

**Altes Residenztheater**
(Cuvilliés-Theater)

**Hofgarten**

**Bavaria mit Ruhmeshalle**
auf der Theresienhöhe

**Schloß Nymphenburg** — Tel. 089/17908-0
Prunk- und Stilräume, Festsaal, Fax 089/17908-627
Schönheitengalerie, Schloß-
kapelle

**Amalienburg, Badenburg, Pa-
godenburg, Magdalenenklause**
im historischen Schloßpark

**Marstallmuseum**
Höfische Kutschen und Schlit-
ten, Reit- und Sattelzeug

**Museum Nymphenburger
Porzellan**
Sammlung Bäuml

| | **Englischer Garten** | Tel. 089/341986 |
| | Landschaftsgarten im | Fax 089/335169 |
| | englischen Stil | |

| München/ | **Neues Schloß Schleißheim** | Tel. 089/315872-0 |
| Oberschleißheim | Festsäle, Staatsappartements, | Fax 089/315872-50 |
| | Gemäldegalerie, barocker Hof- | |
| | garten | |

| | **Schloß Lustheim** | |
| | Porzellansammlung | |

| Neuburg a.d. | **Schloßmuseum** | Tel. 08431/8897 |
| Donau | **Neuburg a.d. Donau** | Fax 08431/42689 |
| | Sgraffitofassade, Kapelle, | |
| | Grotten; Vorgeschichte Pfalz- | |
| | Neuburg, Kirchlicher Barock | |

| Neuschwanstein/ | **Schloß Neuschwanstein** | Tel. 08362/81035 |
| Schwangau | Wohn- und Repräsentations- | und 08362/81801 |
| | räume | Fax 08362/8990 |

| Nürnberg | **Kaiserburg Nürnberg** | Tel. 0911/225726 |
| | Palas, Stilräume, Doppel- | Fax 0911/2059117 |
| | kapelle, Tiefer Brunnen und | |
| | Sinwellturm, Burggarten | |

| Prunn im | **Burg Prunn** | Tel. 09442/3323 |
| Altmühltal | Stilräume | Fax 09442/3335 |

| Riedenburg | **Burg Rosenburg** | Tel. 09442/2752 |
| | Burganlage mit Kapelle; | Fax 09442/3287 |
| | privat betriebener Falkenhof | |

| Schachen | **Königshaus am Schachen** | Tel. 08821/2996 |
| | Wohnräume und Maurischer | |
| | Saal, Alpengarten | |

| Schnaittach | **Festung Rothenberg** | Tel. 09153/7793 |
| | Ruine einer Festungsanlage | |
| | aus dem 18. Jahrhundert | |

| Übersee/Feldwies | **Künstlerhaus Exter** mit Atelier des Malers Julius Exter | Tel. 08642/8950-83<br>Fax 08642/8950-85 |
|---|---|---|
| Utting am Ammersee | **Künstlerhaus Gasteiger**<br>Sommervilla mit Wohnräumen und Werken von Anna und Mathias Gasteiger, Villengarten | Tel. 08806/2682<br>und 08806/2091 |
| Veitshöchheim | **Schloß und Park Veitshöchheim;** Historische Wohnräume, Rokokogarten mit Wasserspielen | Tel. 0931/91582<br>Fax 0931/51925 |
| Würzburg | **Residenz Würzburg;**<br>Barocke Prunkräume, Fresken von G.B. Tiepolo, Gemäldegalerie, Hofgarten | Tel. 0931/355170<br>Fax 0931/51925 |
| | **Festung Marienberg**<br>Festungsanlage, Fürstenbaumuseum mit Schatzkammer, Paramentensaal und stadtgeschichtliche Sammlungen, Maschikuliturm, Fürstengarten; Mainfränkisches Museum | |

# Veröffentlichungen
der Bayerischen Verwaltung der staatlichen Schlösser, Gärten und Seen

**Amtliche Führer**      **je DM 4,00 – 6,00**
**Deutsche Ausgaben:**

| | |
|---|---|
| Ansbach | Residenz Ansbach |
| Aschaffenburg | Schloß Aschaffenburg |
| | Pompejanum in Aschaffenburg |
| | Schloß und Park Schönbusch |
| Bamberg | Neue Residenz Bamberg |
| Bayreuth | Eremitage zu Bayreuth |
| | Markgräfliches Opernhaus Bayreuth |
| | Neues Schloß Bayreuth |
| Bayreuth/Wonsees | Felsengarten Sanspareil – Burg Zwernitz |
| Burghausen | Burg zu Burghausen |
| Coburg | Coburg - Schloß Ehrenburg |
| Coburg/Rödental | Schloß Rosenau |
| Dachau | Schloß Dachau |
| Eichstätt | Willibaldsburg Eichstätt |
| Ellingen | Residenz Ellingen |
| Herrenchiemsee | Neues Schloß Herrenchiemsee |
| Kelheim | Befreiungshalle Kelheim |
| Königssee | St. Bartholomä am Königssee |
| Kulmbach | Plassenburg ob Kulmbach |
| Landshut | Landshut Burg Trausnitz |
| | Stadtresidenz Landshut |
| Lauenstein bei Ludwigsstadt | Burg Lauenstein |
| Linderhof | Schloß Linderhof |
| München | Residenz München |
| | Schatzkammer der Residenz München |
| | Altes Residenztheater in München |
| | (Cuvilliés-Theater) |
| | Englischer Garten München |
| | Ruhmeshalle und Bavaria |
| | Nymphenburg, Schloß, Park und Burgen |
| | Marstallmuseum in Schloß Nymphenburg |
| Neuburg a. d. Donau | Schloßmuseum Neuburg an der Donau |
| Neuschwanstein/Schwangau | Schloß Neuschwanstein |
| Nürnberg | Kaiserburg Nürnberg |
| Oberschleißheim | Schloß Schleißheim, Neues Schloß und Garten |

| | |
|---|---|
| Prunn | Burg Prunn |
| Riedenburg | Burg Rosenburg in Riedenburg an der Altmühl |
| Schachen | Königshaus am Schachen |
| Veitshöchheim | Veitshöchheim |
| Würzburg | Festung Marienberg zu Würzburg Residenz Würzburg und Hofgarten |

**English Editions:**

| | |
|---|---|
| Aschaffenburg | Aschaffenburg Castle |
| Bayreuth | The Hermitage at Bayreuth Margravial Opera House Bayreuth |
| Coburg | Coburg Ehrenburg Palace |
| Herrenchiemsee | The New Palace of Herrenchiemsee |
| Kelheim | The Hall of Liberation at Kelheim |
| Linderhof | Linderhof Palace |
| München | Residence Munich The Treasury in the Munich Residence Nymphenburg, Palace, Park, Pavilions Marstallmuseum Schloß Nymphenburg in Munich |
| Neuschwanstein/Schwangau | Neuschwanstein Castle |
| Nürnberg | Imperial Castle Nuremberg |
| Schachen | The Royal House on the Schachen |
| Würzburg | The Würzburg Residence and Court Gardens |

**Editions with English Summary:**

| | |
|---|---|
| Bamberg | Neue Residenz Bamberg |
| Bayreuth/Wonsees | Felsengarten Sanspareil - Burg Zwernitz |
| Burghausen | Burg zu Burghausen |
| Coburg/Rödental | Schloß Rosenau |
| Königssee | St. Bartholomä am Königssee |
| München | Englischer Garten München |
| Oberschleißheim | Schloß Schleißheim |

**Editions Françaises:**

| | |
|---|---|
| Herrenchiemsee | Le Nouveau Château de Herrenchiemsee |
| Linderhof | Le Château de Linderhof |
| München | Le Trésor de la Résidence de Munich Nymphenburg, Le Château, le Parc et les Pavillons |
| Neuschwanstein/Schwangau | Le Château de Neuschwanstein |

| Nürnberg | Le Château Impérial de Nuremberg |
| Schachen | Le Châlet Royal de Schachen |
| Würzburg | Wurtzbourg, Le Palais des Princes Évêques et les Jardins |

**Editions avec résumé français:**

| Bayreuth/Wonsees | Felsengarten Sanspareil - Burg Zwernitz |
| München | Englischer Garten München |

**Edizioni Italiane:**

| Herrenchiemsee | Castello di Herrenchiemsee |
| Linderhof | Castello di Linderhof |
| München | Tesoro della Residenz München Nymphenburg, II Castello, il Parco e i Castelli del Giardino |
| Neuschwanstein/Schwangau | Castello di Neuschwanstein |
| Würzburg | La Residenza di Würzburg e il Giardino di Corte |

**Japanische Ausgaben:**

| Herrenchiemsee | Schloß Herrenchiemsee |
| Linderhof | Schloß Linderhof |
| München | Nymphenburg |
| Neuschwanstein/Schwangau | Schloß Neuschwanstein |
| Würzburg | Residenz Würzburg und Hofgarten |

## Prospekte und Zeitschriften

| | |
|---|---|
| Prospekt »**Ansbacher Fayencen**« | DM 1,00 |
| Prospekt »**Nymphenburger Porzellan – Sammlung Bäuml**« | DM 1,50 |
| Prospekt »**Residenz Kempten**« (dt., engl.) | DM 2,00 |
| Prospekt »**Schloßpark Linderhof**« | DM 3,00 |
| Prospekt »**Park Schönbusch**« | DM 3,00 |
| Prospekt »**Park Feldafing und Roseninsel**« | DM 3,00 |
| Broschüre »**Staatliche Schlösser und Gärten in Bayern – Besucherinformation 1999**« (deutsch/englisch) | DM 3,00 |

– erhältlich gegen Einsendung von DM 5,– in Briefmarken –

## Museumspädagogische Schriften

**Schloß Nymphenburg entdecken** (1994)            DM 6,00

## Bildhefte der Bayerischen Schlösserverwaltung

Heft 1: *Heym, Sabine:* **Das Alte Residenztheater/Cuvilliés-Theater in München** (dt., engl., frz., ital.); München 1995    DM 15,00

Heft 2: *Heym, Sabine:* **Amadis und Oriane – Im Zauberreich der barocken Oper.** Tapisserien im Neuen Schloß Bayreuth, München 1998    DM 9,00

## Reihe »Forschungen zur Kunst- und Kulturgeschichte«

Band I: *Sangl, Sigrid:* **Das Bamberger Hofschreinerhandwerk im 18. Jahrhundert**; München 1990 (kartoniert)    DM 30,00

Band II: *Hojer, Gerhard:* **Die Prunkappartements Ludwigs I. im Königsbau der Münchner Residenz**; München 1992 (kartoniert)    DM 35,00

Band III: *Stierhof Horst H.:* »**das biblisch gemäl**«. Die Kapelle im Ottheinrichsbau des Schlosses Neuburg an der Donau; München 1993 (broschiert)    DM 12,00

Band IV: *Störkel, Arno:* **Christian Friedrich Carl Alexander. Der letzte Markgraf von Ansbach-Bayreuth**, 2. Auflage, im Bildteil ergänzt und erweitert; Ansbach 1998 (kartoniert)    DM 38,00

Band V: *Hojer, Gerhard* (Hrsg.): **Bayerische Schlösser – Bewahren und Erforschen**; München 1996 (kartoniert)    DM 48,00

Band VI: *Toussaint, Ingo:* **Lustgärten um Bayreuth.** Eremitage, Sanspareil und Fantaisie in Beschreibungen aus dem 18. und 19. Jahrhundert; Georg Olms Verlag, Hildesheim 1998 (kartoniert)    DM 68,00

## Reihe »Baudokumentationen«

o.Nr.: *Land- und Universitätsbauamt Augsburg im Auftrag der Bayerischen Verwaltung der staatlichen Schlösser, Gärten und Seen* (Hrsg.): **Restaurierung Schloß Höchstädt**, Festschrift zur Fertigstellung des I. Bauabschnitts und zur Eröffnung der Fayencenausstellung am 19. Oktober 1995 (broschiert) DM 6,00

o.Nr.: *Landbauamt Rosenheim im Auftrag der Bayerischen Verwaltung der staatlichen Schlösser, Gärten und Seen* (Hrsg.): **Wasserspiele Herrenchiemsee**, Festschrift 1994 (broschiert) DM 15,00

Heft 1: *Staatliches Hochbauamt Weilheim im Auftrag der Bayerischen Verwaltung der staatlichen Schlösser, Gärten und Seen* (Hrsg.): **Das Marokkanische Haus im Schloßpark Linderhof.**
– Band I; Bildheft (broschiert) *ca. DM 15,00*
  *Erscheinungstermin: Herbst 1999*
– Band II; Dokumentation zur Wiedererrichtung
  und Restaurierung (broschiert) · DM 20,00

## Ausstellungskataloge und -Broschüren

*Bayerische Verwaltung der staatlichen Schlösser, Gärten und Seen* (Hrsg.): **200 Jahre Englischer Garten München 1789–1989;** München 1989 (broschiert) DM 4,00

*Bayerische Verwaltung der staatlichen Schlösser, Gärten und Seen* (Hrsg.): **Hortus Eystettensis – ein vergessener Garten?;** München 1999 (broschiert) DM 10,00

*Krückmann, Peter O.* (Bearb.): **Carlo Carlone 1686–1775.** Der Ansbacher Auftrag (kartoniert); Arcos/Landshut 1990 DM 37,00

*Krückmann, Peter O.* (Hrsg.): **Der Himmel auf Erden – Tiepolo in Würzburg.** Band I Ausstellungskatalog. Band II Aufsätze: Prestel, München/New York 1996 (broschiert) Bd. I: DM 39,00 Bd. II: vergriffen

*Krückmann, Peter O.:* **Heaven on Earth – Tiepolo – Masterpieces of the Würzburg Years;** Prestel, München/New York 1996 (broschiert) DM 78,00

*Krückmann, Peter O.:* **Paradies des Rokoko,** Band I Das Bayreuth der Markgräfin Wilhelmine Band II Galli Bibiena und der Musenhof der Wilhelmine von Bayreuth/Ausstellungskatalog; Prestel, München/New York 1998 (Leinen) Bd. I: DM 39,00 Bd. II: DM 39,00 Bd. I+II: DM 69,00

*Schmid, Elmar D.* und *Sabine Heym* (Bearb.): **Josef Effner 1687–1745.** Bauten für Kurfürst Max Emanuel; München 1987 (broschiert) DM 2,00

*Schmid, Elmar D.* (Bearb.): **Friedrich Wilhelm Pfeiffer 1822–1891.** Maler der Reitpferde König Ludwigs II.; Bayerland, Dachau 1988 (kartoniert)| DM 32,00

*Schmid, Elmar D.* und *Sabine Heym* (Bearb.): **Mathias und Anna Gasteiger**. Aus einem Münchner Künstlerleben um 1900; Bayerland, Dachau 1985 (broschiert) · DM 15,00

*Schmid, Elmar D.:* **Der Krönungswagen Kaiser Karls VII**. Wahl und Krönung in Frankfurt am Main 1742; Bayerland, Dachau 1992 (broschiert) · DM 25,00

*Schmid, Elmar D.:* **König Ludwig II. im Portrait**; Bayerland, Dachau 1996 (Leinen) · DM 68,00

*Schmid, Elmar D.:* **Julius Exter – Unbekannte Werke aus dem Nachlaß seiner Schülerin Olga Fritz-Zetter**; München 1996 (broschiert) · DM 10,00

*Schmid, Elmar D.:* **Julius Exter – Aufbruch in die Moderne**; Klinkhardt & Biermann, München/Berlin 1998 (broschiert) · DM 48,00

*Stierhof, Horst H.:* **»das biblisch gemäl«**. 450 Jahre Schloßkapelle Neuburg an der Donau; München 1993 (broschiert) · DM 5,00

## Bestandskataloge

*Frosien-Leinz, Heike* und *Ellen Weski* (Bearb.): **Das Antiquarium der Münchner Residenz**, Katalog der Skulpturen. 2 Bände; Hirmer, München 1987 (Leinen)
*– nur im Buchhandel erhältlich –*

*Helmberger, Werner* und *Valentin Kockel* (Bearb.): **Rom über die Alpen tragen**. Fürsten sammeln antike Architektur. Die Aschaffenburger Korkmodelle; Arcos, Landshut 1993 (kartoniert) · DM 29,00

*Hojer, Gerhard* (Hrsg.): **König Ludwig II.-Museum Herrenchiemsee, Katalog**; Hirmer, München 1986 (kartoniert) · DM 35,00

*Langer, Brigitte:* **Die Möbel der Residenz München, Band 1**. Die französischen Möbel des 18. Jahrhunderts, hrsg. von Gerhard Hojer und Hans Ottomeyer; Prestel, München/New York 1995 (broschiert) · DM 118,00
*(Buchhandelspreis/Leinen: DM 228,00)*

*Langer, Brigitte* und *Alexander Herzog von Württemberg:* **Die Möbel der Residenz München, Band 2**. Die deutschen Möbel des 16. bis 18. Jahrhunderts, hrsg. von Gerhard Hojer und Hans Ottomeyer; Prestel, München/New York 1996 (broschiert) · DM 118,00
*(Buchhandelspreis/Leinen: DM 228,00)*

*Langer, Brigitte, Hans Ottomeyer* und *Alexander Herzog von Württemberg:* **Die Möbel der Residenz München, Band 3**. Möbel des Empire, Biedermeier und Spätklassizismus, hrsg. von Gerhard Hojer und Hans Ottomeyer; Prestel, München/New York 1997 (broschiert) · DM 118,00
*(Buchhandelspreis/Leinen: DM 228,00)*

*Miller, Albrecht* (Bearb.): **Bayreuther Fayencen;** Arcos,
Landshut 1994 (kartoniert)                                    DM 28,00
*Seelig, Lorenz:* **Kirchliche Schätze aus bayerischen Schlössern.**
Liturgische Gewände und Geräte des 16. bis 19. Jahrhunderts;
Deutscher Kunstverlag, Berlin 1984 (broschiert)               DM 10,00
*Ziffer, Alfred:* **Nymphenburger Porzellan.** Die Sammlung Bäuml/
Bäuml Collection; Arnoldsche, Stuttgart 1996 (broschiert)     DM 98,00

## Weitere Veröffentlichungen

*Albert, Jost und Werner Helmberger:* **Der Landschaftsgarten
Schönbusch bei Aschaffenburg;** Wernersche, Worms 1999
(kartoniert)                                                  DM 36,00
*Bayerische Verwaltung der staatlichen Schlösser, Gärten und Seen*
(Hrsg.): **Vierte Festschrift zum Wiederaufbau der Residenz
München;** München 1959 (broschiert)                         DM 5,00
*Bayerische Verwaltung der staatlichen Schlösser, Gärten und Seen*
(Hrsg.): **Journal der Bayerischen Verwaltung der staatlichen
Schlösser Gärten und Seen;** München 1995 (broschiert)       DM 10,00
*Ermischer, Gerhard:* **Schloßarchäologie – Funde zu Schloß
Johannisburg in Aschaffenburg;** Museen der Stadt Aschaffen-
burg/Bayerische Schlösserverwaltung, Aschaffenburg 1996
(kartoniert)                                                  DM 48,00
*Facharbeitskreis Schlösser und Gärten in Deutschland (Hrsg.):*
**Reisezeit – Zeitreise zu den schönsten Schlössern, Burgen,
Gärten, Klöstern und Römerbauten in Deutschland;** Schnell &
Steiner, Regensburg 1999 (broschiert)                        DM 16,80
– auch in englisch und französisch erhältlich –
*Focht, Josef:* **Die musische Aura der Markgräfin Wilhelmine.**
Musikinszenierung in der Kunst des Bayreuther Rokoko;
Peda, Passau 1998 (broschiert)                               DM 17,80
*Focht, Josef* und *Hans Gurski:* **Das Gloria der Engel im Fürststift
Kempten.** Musikdarstellungen in der Basilika St. Lorenz und
der Residenz; Peda, Passau 1998 (broschiert)                DM 17,80
*Heym, Sabine:* **Feenreich und Ritterwelt – Die Rosenau als Ort
romantisch-literarischen Welterlebens.** Sonderdruck aus
»Bayerische Schlösser – Bewahren und Erforschen«;
München 1996 (broschiert)                                    DM 4,00
*Hojer, Gerhard* (Hrsg.): **Der Italienische Bau.** Materialien
und Untersuchungen zur Stadtresidenz Landshut;
Arcos, Landshut 1994 (kartoniert)                            DM 38,00

*Hojer, Gerhard* und *Peter O. Krückmann:* **Neues Schloß Bayreuth, Anton Raphael Mengs:** »**Königin Semiramis erhält die Nachricht vom Aufstand in Babylon**« (PATRIMONIA 49); Kulturstiftung der Länder und Bayerische Schlösserverwaltung, Berlin/München 1995 (broschiert)      DM 20,00

*Kunz-Ott, Hannelore* und *Andrea Kluge* (Hrsg.): **150 Jahre Feldherrnhalle.** Lebensraum einer Großstadt; Buchendorfer, München 1994 (broschiert)      DM 25,00

*Kutschbach, Doris:* **Tiepolo – Eine Reise um die Welt** (aus der Kinderbuch-Reihe »Abenteuer Kunst«); Prestel, München/New York 1996 (kartoniert)      DM 22,80

*Langer, Brigitte:* **Residenz München, zwei Kommoden des Bernard II Vanrisamburgh** (PATRIMONIA 134); Kulturstiftung der Länder und Bayerische Schlösserverwaltung, Berlin/München 1997 (broschiert)      DM 20,00

*Lauterbach, Iris, Klaus Endemann und Christoph Luitpold Frommel* (Hrsg.): **Die Landshuter Stadtresidenz.** Architektur und Ausstattung; Zentralinstitut für Kunstgeschichte (Band XIV), München 1998 (broschiert)      DM 48,00

*Misslbeck-Woesler, Maria:* **Die Flora des Englischen Gartens, München 1986** (kartoniert)      DM 15,00

*Nickl, Peter* (Hrsg.): **Parkett.** Historische Holzfußböden und zeitgenössische Parkettkultur; Klinkhardt & Biermann, München/Berlin 1995 (Leinen)      DM 78,00

*Schmid, Elmar D.:* **Das Exter-Haus** – Ein Künstlersitz am Chiemsee in Übersee-Feldwies; München 1997 (broschiert)      DM 10,00

*Schuster, Rainer:* **Nymphenburger Porzellan.** Kostbarkeiten aus der Sammlung Bäuml und dem Residenzmuseum München; München 1997 (broschiert)      DM 8,00

*Schuster, Rainer:* **Nymphenburg Porcelain.** Treasures from the Bäuml Collection and the Residence Museum Munich; München 1997 (broschiert)      DM 8,00

*Stierhof, Horst H.* (Bearb.): **Das Walhnhaus.** Der italienische Bau der Stadtresidenz Landshut; Landshut 1994 (broschiert)      DM 16,00

*Werner, Ferdinand:* **Der Hofgarten Veitshöchheim;** Wernersche, Worms 1998 (kartoniert)      DM 36,00

# Plakate

*groß (A 1):*

| | |
|---|---|
| **Schlösserland** Bayern | DM 7,00 |
| **König Ludwig II.** (Portrait von Ferdinand Piloty, 1865) | DM 7,00 |
| **Nymphenburger Porzellan** – Sammlung Bäuml | DM 7,00 |
| **Marstallmuseum** | DM 7,00 |
| **Residenz München** | DM 7,00 |
| **Schatzkammer** der Residenz München | DM 7,00 |
| **Schloß Rosenau** | DM 7,00 |
| **Schloß Ehrenburg** Coburg | DM 7,00 |
| **Schloß** und **Park Schönbusch** | DM 7,00 |
| **Bayreuther Fayencen** (Sammlung Rummel) | DM 7,00 |
| Landshut: **Burg Trausnitz** – **Stadtresidenz** | DM 7,00 |
| **Residenz Kempten** | DM 7,00 |
| **»Rom über die Alpen tragen«** (Korkmodelle in Schloß Johannisburg) | DM 5,00 |
| **Schloßmuseum Neuburg an der Donau** | DM 5,00 |

*klein (A 2/A 3)*

| | |
|---|---|
| Korkmodell **»Pantheon«** (Schloß Johannisburg) | DM 5,00 |
| **Pompejanum** Aschaffenburg | DM 5,00 |
| **Neue Residenz Bamberg** | DM 5,00 |
| Plan **»Schloßpark Nymphenburg«** | DM 5,00 |
| Ausstellungsplakat **»das biblisch gemäl«** (Schloßkapelle Neuburg) | DM 3,00 |
| Ausstellungsplakat **»von denen schönen Gärten«** (Schloß Fantaisie) | DM 5,00 |
| Ausstellungsplakat **»Hortus Eystettensis«** (Willibaldsburg Eichstätt) | DM 5,00 |
| Ausstellungsplakat **»Alles scheint Natur…«** (Park Schönbusch) | DM 5,00 |

## CD-ROM

**Ludwig II. – Ich, der König.**
Leben, Schlösser, Musik, Dynastie, Zeitgeschichte | DM 79,00
**Ludwig II – I, the king.**
Life, Castles, Music, Dynasty, Contemporary History | DM 79,00

## Videos des Bayerischen Rundfunks

– **Nymphenburg, Schloß und Park** (PAL/dt.; NTSC/engl.) | DM 39,95
– **Die Kaiserburg in Nürnberg** (PAL/dt.) | DM 39,95
– **Die Königsschlösser** (PAL/dt., PAL/engl.; NTSC/engl.) | DM 39,95
Das Video »Die Königsschlösser« gibt es in englischer
Sprache in zwei verschiedenen Systemen: im PAL-System
(z.B. für Großbritannien und Südafrika) und im
NTSC-System (z.B. für USA, Kanada und Japan).
– **»Herr der sieben Länder« – Kurfürst Carl Theodor
von Baiern und der Pfalz** (PAL/dt.) | DM 29,95

## Ausstellungsvideos:

– **»Der Himmel auf Erden«** – Tiepolo in der Würzburger
Residenz | DM 39,95
– **»Das vergessene Paradies«** – Galli Bibiena und der
Musenhof der Wilhelmine von Bayreuth | DM 29,95

**Preise zzgl. Porto und Verpackung,
Bestellungen bitte an:
Bayerische Verwaltung der
staatlichen Schlösser, Gärten und Seen
Postfach 38 01 20, 80614 München
Tel: 089/17908-165; Fax 089/17908-154**